KATHMANDU

Photographs by Dominic Sansoni
Text by Jim Goodman

Designed by Leonard Lueras

Time Books International
New Delhi

This page: *Bhaktapur has its own Kumari; although less-renowned than her Kathmandu counterpart, she still plays an important ritual role during the annual Dasain Festival.* ***Following pages:*** *Nepalese devotees carry Kumari to view the annual Horse Festival; Tibetan novices enjoy a happy moment in the Boudhanath monastery; and, breathtaking views of the world's greatest mountain range, are just a few days' trek from Kathmandu along picturesque routes.*

CONTENTS

VALLEY OF THE GODS
Pages 13 – 61

Historical Chronology
page 24

Dealing with Demons
page 33

Sex and the Lightning Goddess
page 38

Pomp in Another Circumstance
page 44

The Private Life of an Ex-Goddess
page 49

Carpets for Dharma: The Tibetans
page 58

BACK OF THE BOOK
Pages 63 – 104

Valley Map
page 64

Valley Trivia
page 66

Best Bets
page 68

Valley Tours
page 75

Treks
page 88

Off the Beaten Trek
page 92

Travel Notes
page 96

Index
page 104

Kathmandu
Valley of the Gods

One refrain invariably runs through introductory rides through the dusty streets and alleys of Kathmandu: "It's so medieval here!" The words roll off visiting tongues, a reflex action to the kaleidoscope of sights, sounds and smells that greet the senses everywhere like vignettes and paintings from a history book on the Middle Ages come to life.

All is not mired in the past, however. Travelers fly in and out, they stay and eat at places equipped with all the latest conveniences, and they find everything from videos to ice cream are available. There's plenty of traffic congestion, too. Cars, motorbikes, animals and people all maneuver through the same narrow passageways usually at the same time. The shrill blasts of Japanese vehicle horns and high-pitched squeals of Indian-made trucks bounce off the high walls of houses built flush to the street; the sheer intensity of all the noise is much harder on the ears than the sounds in cities that are bigger and more spread out than Kathmandu.

Yet even that problem harks back centuries, to an age when urban planning did not have to cater to motor vehicles. Religious precepts governed the layout then. In fact many streets are still punctuated by shrines, temples, sacred stones and sunken baths. Vehicular traffic grinds to a halt because of a slow-roaming bull, a long procession of devotees, or a wheelcart with a load that's much too wide. At times, it's impossible to determine whether the contemporary has intruded upon the medieval, or vice versa.

One thing is certain, however: under Kathmandu's modern integument, beats an ancient heart. That pulse courses through the city's arteries as surely as tiered temple tops dominate the landscapes. When strolling through the brick lanes, the judicious keep one eye out for things flung without warning from upper story windows and one eye on the pits and protrusions of the street, dodging the occasional scavenger dog, chicken or bull.

Children dash by dragging their siblings on a little homemade chariot. A pair of Newar farmer girls in red-bordered black sarees, carrying trays of powders and grains for *puja* rites, duck into a temple courtyard. Street hawkers saunter by brandishing cheap textiles from India, fruits from the Terai, straw mats, stuffed mongooses; on

the town squares they sit beside displays of ready-made clothing, cosmetics, medicinal herbs, and baskets of fruit and vegetables.

In shops, goods are piled into bins and sacks instead of tin cans and plastic packages. At the next square, there's an itinerant show in town: a boy and his cobra, a man and his trained bear, a magician and his son. During the harvest season, Kathmandu's streets are filled with drying chilies, mustard, wheat and rice. In another season, it's festival time and the city is filled with people tingling with anticipation.

The sound of approaching flutes, drums and cymbals rises above the din. The

Children honor the Black Bhairab *of Hanuman Dhoka; tradition says those who swear false oaths in its presence will vomit blood and die* **(left).** *The divine couple, Shiva and Parvati, gaze from the window of a Durbar Square temple* **(above).**

13

procession that arrives is not one of those slow, reverent walks with a pacific deity, but a chaotic romp with Bhairab or a mother-goddess. The god is rocked down the street on a stately palanquin in fits and starts and bursts of speed. Another day, another procession.

Long lines of enthusiasts grip thick ropes hauling an antique chariot. It's stuck. They jerk it forward and it careens down the lane, lopping off an awning and smashing in a store front en route. Spectators scatter to the porches while the neighborhood lunatic, oblivious to the excitement, daubs someone's forehead and hands him a withered flower petal. If it's not a deity on a chariot, it may be a troupe of masked dancers with fierce eyes, bright fangs and swords, accompanied by the whine of fleugelots and the polyrhythmic thumps of the drums. Even today, such rituals are not mere performances trotted out for groups of gawking tourists after a buffet dinner. In the Kathmandu Valley, extraordinary spectacle is still an ordinary part of life.

A devotee makes an offering to an image of Vishnu sleeping in the coils of the serpent Sesha **(above)**. This ancient stone masterpiece lies in a pond at Budhanilkantha at the foot of Shivapuri Mountain, nine kilometers north of Kathmandu.

With a population of only 300,000, Kathmandu is atypical of other teeming capitals of Asia. But if it pales beside them in size, it overwhelms them in the beauty of its setting. Kathmandu lies at the confluence of the Vishnumati and Bagmati, rivers that are mere streams in winter but turn into torrents in summer, in a sprawling, hill-bounded valley with rolling richly-colored contours and an awesome snow-capped mountain backdrop.

Kathmandu is flanked south of the Bagmati by Patan which is about a third as large but centuries older. Patan was a great Buddhist center in ancient times. Its proximity to the capital spawned the growth of modern suburbs, yet it retains a traditional look in its old town. Patan is replete with monasteries and mottled with *stupas*, ponds, *chaityas* and statues; history and mystery beckon from a thousand doorways.

To the east stands Bhaktapur, the third of what were once a trio of independent, quarreling states. It's just distant enough from the others to have developed a special character of its own and to escape some of the modern influences that have swamped Kathmandu and Patan. In fact, it's practically a self-contained unit: Bhaktapur's original medieval layout remains largely intact; its population comprises mainly conservative Newar farmers; and, its infrastructure and artistic and architectural heritage have been restored by a 13-year, German-sponsored development project.

The rest of the Kathmandu Valley is dappled by smaller towns and villages scattered around scalloped fields, hillocks and climbing terraces. Patches of forest persist, growing thicker on the slopes of the big hills. The Valley's rim is still infested with wild animals which, while protected by law, often escape the walled boundaries of the forest reserves. Boars still ravage crops, and leopards kidnap domestic animals. Tigers rule the hinterland. The howl of jackals and the plaintive cry of barking deer rent the rural night air. And snakes slither through the fields and over the paths in the thick green months of summer.

Few cities change with the seasons as dramatically as Kathmandu. Winter is marked by the morning fog, early spring by swatches of yellow mustard fields and the budding trees and flowers on Kantipath, and late spring by the threshing and stacking of wheat in the lanes and squares. Gray skies and rain come with the early monsoon, then great bursts of green fields and squares laden with red chilies are telltale signs that summer is ending. Autumn brings back the snow peaks and bathes the Valley in the golden sheen of ripening paddy. Late autumn leaves piles of rice in the streets, winnowed and dried by day, slept on by kids at night.

Most of life's daily routines occur in the open in the Kathmandu Valley. That makes it particularly charming and attractive for visitors. Grains and vegetables, dried by

turns in the squares and courtyards, provide insights into how the free use of public space compensates for the congestion of living quarters. You'll see boisterous good cheer bubble from long rows of men and women planting or reaping in the fields as they socialize, exchange jokes, flirt and share a collective meal. During the construction season, you can watch groups of men erect bamboo scaffolds, haul and pass bricks and timber.

On the domestic side, you'll see women engaged in the drudgery of washing, cleaning, water-fetching and even yarn-winding with friends and relatives. After their

*Morning fog shrouds the morning ablutions on the Bagmati River at Pashupatinath **(above)**, the most sacred shrine in the kingdom. The gilt-roofed Rajeswari Temple compound is also built on the wooded bank of the sacred river **(following pages)**.*

15

chores, women sit outdoors on the porches or in the resthouses, picking the lice from each other's hair, giving dry-season mustard oil massages, stitching the children's clothes or just chatting.

Most of the non-field work is conducted around the home, too, at leisure — and with frequent interruptions. In Bhaktapur, the shuttles of handlooms can be heard clacking inside scores of houses. Near

Swayambhunath and Boudhanath, carpet weavers tie and pound threads into place. Potters in Thimi and Bhaktapur spin their wheels and fashion their vessels outdoors while painters and jewelers work in the ground floor shops of their houses. Elsewhere, herders lead their animals on buses to the markets. In the morning, butchers dump the headless, slaughtered carcasses of buffalos into the streets and light a straw fire beside them to burn off the hair.

Like virtually every other facet of life, religion is also a public affair. Unlike most other countries in which people usually pray inside houses of worship, devotees in

On a cobbled square in old Bhaktapur, a Newar farmer totes his fresh garden produce to the market **(above)** and women return home carrying bowls of fresh curd for the evening meal **(right)**. Curd is one of the favorite local refreshments.

Nepal usually do *puja* outside. You'll see people ringing bells, lighting lamps, tossing grains, coins and petals and applying vermilion paste to the forehead of a stone or wooden deity, or pasting a food offering across its mouth. The predominant religious influence in the Kathmandu Valley, as it is throughout Nepal, is Hinduism. By strict definition, Hindu *puja* is a form of entertaining God as a royal guest. The festive activities, constant offerings, and occasional sacrificial slaughter of animals surround the adoration of images that represent various manifestations of God. Originally, these ceremonies were held to purify, protect, and resuscitate nature and the community. Today, they are as much a form of entertainment as of worship.

Processions crowd the streets: a deity in a palanquin, a marriage band, a private family or caste observance, a masked dance making the rounds, or a whole neighborhood carrying trays of food balanced on each end of the bamboo pole to the fields for a ritual feast. The last pole-carrier balances his baby son on one tray, the neighborhood god on the other! Although the heads of the statues of deities have been rubbed smooth during centuries of solemn handling, it's still possible to identify each god by its distinctive set of weapons, conveyances, and by postures repeated again and again in statues, carvings, paintings and illustrations; it would be difficult for a Nepalese to grow up unaware of any but the most esoteric.

Consequently, symbols permeate the Nepalese environment. They are chiseled in stone, carved in wood, cast in metal, pounded out in sheets, painted on walls and clay pots, and even illustrate comic books. They cover windows, doorways, brackets, posts, rest houses, and courtyards as well as temples. Some are not even religious in nature and include a veritable menagerie of animals or vignettes of everyday experiences like field work, feasting, music, dance, the apparition of demons, and, of course, that most universal of preoccupations, sex. Like Gothic cathedrals, the public buildings reflect the facts and fantasies of daily life.

These symbols are part of a pervasive religious spirit that extends to the recognition of house and field deities and regulates an almost continuous round of worship duties that include rites for frogs, snakes, dogs, crows, cows and bulls as well as the obvious deities. Religion inspires the ornate decorations of votive objects. It sanctifies nature; there are cults involving rivers, trees, stones and mountains. It clothes each year in familiar attire. Every agricultural season, indeed almost every turn of the plow, has its ritual; even the performance of mundane annual chores are exalted in festivals.

Pujas and festivals are great social

affairs, a time to dress up and renew old ties with friends and kin, a time when the young flirt while their parents scout "suitable" marriage partners before the flirting goes too far. The celebrations also promote a national identity and unity: the spectacle attracts every race and religion and familiarity with different customs breeds respect. In Nepal, Hindus call on Buddhist divinities as well as their own; Buddhists, likewise, honor Hindu gods. Mutual respect and tolerance have characterized religion in Nepal since its inception and the nation is proud of the fact that religious conflicts have never marred its history.

In central Nepal's Pokhara Valley, *a family rows to market across the placid morning waters of Phewa Lake* **(left).** *During Kathmandu's dry winter months, dense fog envelops the city streets on most mornings making for a moody stroll* **(above).**

Historical Chronology

c. BC 700 — Kiratas from the Eastern Himalayas invade the Valley and establish a state.

c. BC 560 — Birth of Siddhartha Gautama, the historical Buddha, in Lumbini, an area that today is part of the Nepalese Terai.

BC 250 — The Mauryan Emperor Ashoka visits Lumbini and raises an inscribed pillar to commemorate the occasion. Nepalese legend asserts that the emperor also visited Patan at this time and constructed five *stupas* in and around the city. He is said to have left his daughter Charumati here to marry a Deopatan prince. She is credited with building the monastery that bears her name in the town of Chabahil.

c. AD 200 — The Kiratas succumb to the new Somabansi Dynasty which introduces the Hindu caste system that still influences society today.

c. AD 300 — Lichhavis from North India enter the Valley to found a new dynasty.

464 — Manadeva I celebrates his martial victories by inscribing his accomplishments on a stone pillar at Changu Narayan. His account becomes Nepal's oldest extant historical record.

605–21 — Reign of the non-Lichhavi Amsuvarman, who earned a reputation as a great builder and patron of the arts.

639 — The Kuti Pass to Tibet opens. Around this time, say the annals, Princess Bhrikuti marries Tibet's King Srongtsan Gampo. She and her Chinese co-wife convert the King to Buddhism.

643 — Narendradeva I (643–679) establishes relations with the Tang court of China. Tang emissary Wang Hsuan-tse passes through Nepal enroute to India and writes the earliest eyewitness account of the country's artistic and commercial wealth.

647 — Wang is insulted by the new King of Kanauj and returns to Nepal, enlists Nepalese military aid and avenges the insult.

733 — Jayadeva II dies and Lichhavi rule effectively comes to an end signaling the start of Nepal's Dark Ages, an era of scanty historical records and a welter of competing dynastic lines.

879 — Ragavadeva Laxmi founds a new state and initiates a new calendar era called the Nepal Sambat. Each new year begins on the first day following the new moon between October and

Portraits depict a young King Tribhuvan dressed in ceremonial robes (left) and Jung Bahadur Rana, posing with one of his wives about 1860, (right) on the preceding pages. Below, Durbar Square, Kathmandu, in the 1850s (left) and Jayaprakash, the last king of Malla (right).

November. Although Ragavadeva's dynasty does not last long, his calendar is still used by the major ethnic group, the Newars, today.

949 — The man traditionally regarded as the founder of Kathmandu, Gunakamadeva I, accedes to the throne. In addition to creating a unified state, he is also credited with establishing its Indrajatra, Krishna Jayanti and Machhendranath festivals.

1024 — The reign of Laxmikamadeva begins. He inaugurates the cult of the Living Goddess Kumari.

1040 — The influential Bengali Tantric Buddhist monk Dipankara visits the Valley and contributes to the flowering of Nepalese monasticism.

1147–66 — Reign of Anandeva I, who makes Bhaktapur his capital.

1200 — The last Thakuri state falls and the first Malla Dynasty begins.

1244–1311 — Mithila invaders from south of Nepal lay waste to the Valley and plunder its towns and temples during the course of at least five raids.

1255 — A major earthquake kills one-third of Nepal's population.

1260 — At the invitation of the new Mongol Emperor Kublai Khan, a team of Nepalese artisans under the direction of Arniko departs for Tibet to construct a monastery for the Khan's Tibetan guru. Arniko later works in Beijing and builds the still-extant White Pagoda.

1287–1344 — Khasa warriors from western Nepal carry out six raids on the Valley but, being devout Buddhists, spare the holy places.

1326 — Muslim armies destroy the state of Mithila and its prince, Harisimhadeva, flees to Nepal. He dies on the way but his widow Devaladevi, who may have been the sister of the Malla king Rudra, presses on to Bhaktapur. There, her extraordinary talents mature to the point where she becomes the prime manipulator behind the throne and the acknowledged de facto ruler, the most powerful woman ever to walk the stage of Nepalese politics.

1344 — The first Malla Dynasty ends with Rudra's death which has a divisive effect on the Valley.

1346 — Muslims under Sultan Shamsuddin of Bengal attack the Valley for an entire week, looting all the towns and temples except Changu Narayan and Sankhu. After the holocaust, petty chieftains and bandit gangs compete for territory. A second Malla line clings to power in Patan.

1354 — Devaladevi arranges the marriage of her granddaughter Rajalladevi to her protégé Jayasthiti Malla in an attempt to regain power.

1366 — Devaladevi dies, but Jayasthiti's marriage has given him a claim to the throne. His position is so secure that by 1370 he effectively becomes the ruler of the country.

1382 — Jayasthiti's last political opponent succumbs to the inevitable and crowns Jayasthiti King of Nepal. The third and most important Malla Dynasty commences. The new monarch suppresses the bandit gangs and reorganizes the administration of state and society. Apparently, existing customs are codified and include carefully-graded distinctions in dress and residence, as well as the duties, of the many caste groups.

1395 — Jayasthiti dies but his three sons share power successfully and the new regime continues.

1428 — Yakshya Malla accedes to the throne and extends the kingdom beyond the Valley. He also establishes the precedent for lavish court patronage of religion and the arts.

1482 — Yakshya dies and the realm is divided among his children.

1484 — Ratna Malla establishes Kathmandu as an independent kingdom. From now on the Mallas are in perpetual rivalry and periods of amity among the three kingdoms are rare.

1560–79 — Mahendra Malla reigns. He builds a splendid temple to Taleju Bhavani, visits the Mughal Emperor Humayun in Delhi and initiates the use of silver coins.

1618–58 — Siddhi Narsingh Malla reigns in Patan and becomes noted as the city's most illustrious builder of elaborate temples.

1628 — The first known visit of a European to Nepal. The Portuguese João Cabral passes through enroute to Bengal from Shigatse.

1641–74 — Pratap Malla reigns in Kathmandu. As a renowned builder, poet, lover and polylinguist, he leads the city to the peak of its power.

1685 — The state of Gorkha interferes in the politics of the Valley for the first time when it signs a treaty with Kathmandu and Bhaktapur that pits the three cities against Patan.

1696–1722 — Bhupatindra Malla reigns in Bhaktapur. He becomes an accomplished poet and playwright, who lavishes money on the arts. He also builds Nyatapola, the tallest and most graceful example of Nepalese pagoda-style architecture.

1707 — Capuchin missionaries pass through enroute to Lhasa and write the earliest European description of the Valley.

1716 — Bhupatindra grants the Capuchins permission to establish themselves in Bhaktapur.

1719 — About 20,000 people die as plague ravages the cities and towns of the Valley.

1734 — Accession of Jayaprakash Malla, the last of his line to rule Kathmandu. Because of his unfortunate penchant for making enemies, Jayaprakash gradually alienates most of his subjects. He and his rivals in Bhaktapur and Patan become so involved in their mutual antagonisms that they fail to recognize the ambitions of the Gorkha prince Prithvinarayan Shah, despite the latter's long and concerted campaign against them.

1744 — Nuwakot falls to the Gorkhalis and Prithvinarayan is now in position to blockade the Valley.

1768 — Prithvinarayan marches into Kathmandu on Indrajatra day. The Malla king's troops are preparing to celebrate the drawing of Kumari's chariot and are too drunk to resist. Jayaprakash flees to Patan and later to Bhaktapur. Seeing Prithvinarayan firmly in control in Kathmandu, the Pradhans of Patan turn over their city to him while their king escapes to Bhaktapur.

1769 — After failing to strike a deal with King Ranjit Malla, Prithvinarayan attacks Bhaktapur. The city puts up a stiff resistance but finally falls, marking the end of the Malla Era. Jayaprakash is mortally wounded and Ranjit permitted to retire to Benares. The victory establishes the Shah Dynasty, the same one that presently holds power. Prithvinarayan moves his capital to Kathmandu after having unified and consolidated Nepal.

1774 — Prithvinarayan dies. For his role in uniting the country and laying the foundations of the modern kingdom of Nepal, he becomes known as the "Father of the Nation."

1787–92 — Encroachments by Gurkhas into Sikkim and Tibet lead to war with China. The Gurkhas suffer defeat and by the terms of the subsequent treaty are required to send tribute to China every five years. The treaty also terminates Nepal's northern expansionist ambitions.

1791 — Nepal, as a consequence of military failures on the northern front, signs a commercial treaty with the British East India Company. Later that year Nepal applies for assistance.

1792 — Colonel Kirkpatrick arrives in Kathmandu only to find that under the treaty just signed with China, Nepal no longer has any need for military assistance. However, Kirkpatrick's report survives as an important historical source for the period.

1795 — Nepalese troops overrun and annex Garwhal and Kumaon in the Western Himalayas.

1801 — In a maneuver against its rivals, a faction of the Nepalese court signs a commercial treaty with the East India Company.

1802 — Captain W.D. Knox is appointed British Resident and arrives to take up his post. But the Nepalese side does not abide by the terms of the treaty and Knox is withdrawn a year later.

1804 — Lord Wellesley strikes back by unilaterally abrogating the 1801 treaty.

1806 — The political career of Bhimsen Thapa commences. For the next three decades he wields near absolute authority as Prime Minister.

1814 — Encroachments by Gurkhas on British-held territory lead to war.

1816 — General Ochterlony advances to Makwanpur and forces Nepalese capitulation. By the terms of the Treaty of 1816 Nepal surrenders Garwhal, Kumaon, Darjeeling and recently-acquired portions of the Terai. A British Resident takes up permanent posting in Kathmandu. While they are ultimately victorious, the British are so impressed with the fighting skills of their opponents that they arrange for their recruitment into their own forces, thus originating the world-famous Gurkha brigades, much respected for their fighting prowess even today.

1833 — A huge earthquake devastates the Valley.

1837 — Fall of Bhimsen Thapa.

1839 — Nepal signs an agreement with the East India Company not to conduct business with Indian states except through the company offices.

1846 — Court factionalism peaks with the assassination of a royal favorite. Jung Bahadur Rana engineers the assembly of hundreds of his political enemies under the pretext of discussing the crisis. He then has them all murdered in the infamous Kot massacre, and takes control of the country. Thus begins the Rana Era during which the Shah monarchs are kept in seclusion under virtual house arrest while the reigns of power are in the hands of Jung Bahadur Rana and his relatives.

The newly-crowned King Mahendra acknowledges his nation's salute in 1955 (below). Following pages: King Mahendra strides into Basantapur Palace (left); Shanker Shumsher (top right) and Colonel Chandra Jung Thapa (bottom right) pose with trophies after a hunt at Chitwan early this century.

1850–51 — Jung Bahadur Rana makes a state visit to Great Britain. When he returns to Nepal, he institutes a liberal revision of the criminal code. He also inaugurates the wearing of European dress at court and the building of European-style palatial dwellings with imported materials with the first of the Rana palaces.

1854–56 — Border and trading disputes with Tibet lead to clashes at Kuti Pass. In the resulting treaties, Tibet is required to pay an annual indemnity of Rs 10,000 and acknowledges Nepalese commercial rights in Lhasa.

1857–58 — Jung Bahadur Rana dispatches military assistance to the British during the Indian mutiny. In gratitude, the British return a portion of the western Terai to Nepal, the last territorial change in the country to date.

1877 — Jung Bahadur Rana dies. His successor, Rana Uddip, suppresses a royal attempt by the Shahs to regain power.

1884 — The royal family is removed to the newly-constructed Narayan Hity Palace.

1885 — Bir Shumsher Rana assassinates Rana Uddip, makes himself Prime Minister, and excludes Jung Bahadur's line from the succession.

1901 — Chandra Shumser's career as Prime Minister begins. Singha Durbar is built.

1914 — Chandra Shumser sends Gurkhas to fight for the Allies' World War I campaign in Europe.

1923 — Great Britain revises the 1816 Treaty of Sagauli and recognizes Nepal's independence.

1934 — A massive earthquake levels most of Nepal's built-up area and kills thousands.

1939–45 — Over 300,000 Nepalese participate in World War II, both as regular Gurkha brigades of the British Army and as attached units from the Nepalese Army.

1947 — India achieves independence, arousing the hopes of democratic forces in Nepal. A major struggle against the Rana autocracy commences.

1950 — Chinese troops occupy Tibet, nullifying its treaty arrangements with Nepal. Demonstrations against the Rana regime spread. King Tribhuvan escapes from custody and with great fanfare is granted asylum in India.

1951 — With India's backing, King Tribhuvan returns to Kathmandu and leads the overthrow of the Rana autocracy. Nepal reopens its borders.

1953 — Tenzing Norgay and Edmund Hillary become the first men to set foot on the peak of Mt. Everest. Dozens of expeditions follow.

1955 — Accession of King Mahendra. The Dalai and Panchen Lamas, in a rare joint appearance outside Tibet, are among the guests at the coronation. Nepal joins the United Nations.

1959 — Tibet's Dalai Lama flees to India. Attempting to follow, thousands of Tibetans enter Nepal.

1962 — King Mahendra introduces the Panchayat system of government, a form of village democracy in which he appoints a prime minister to preside over a partyless 140-member National Legislative Assembly. He also inaugurates a program aimed at beautifying the shabby city.

1968 — Young westerners stream into Nepal in search of a spiritual nirvana on earth, bringing Kathmandu international notoriety as a popular, if unwilling, hub for the era's hippy peace movement.

1972 — Mahendra dies and absolute power passes to his son, the current reigning sovereign, His Majesty King Birendra Bir Bikram Shah. He soon declares that one of the major objectives of his foreign policy is to win international recognition for Nepal as a Zone of Peace.

1980 — In a national referendum, a majority of the country's adult voters choose to retain the Panchayat system of government rather than switch to a more democratic Western form of government.

The best way to acquire an instant appreciation of the legend of Nepal's creation is to climb one of its highest hills during winter to watch the sun rise. Although dense fog swathes the Kathmandu Valley at dawn, the golden-spired stupa of Swayambhunath pokes high enough above the steamy waves to catch the first rays of the sun.

According to local legend, in the begin-

ning the cloud was a lake; Swayambhunath an island. One day the sage Viswapa sat down atop Nagarjung and pitched a lotus seed into the waters that floated to the island and it bloomed. From the petals burst forth a flame that cast a light across the lake. The hero of Nepalese lore, Manjusri, recognized that the flame was the handiwork of the primordial Adi-Buddha, so he wanted to worship it. Unable to find a way to the island across the waters, he slashed the wall of rock with his sword and the waters flowed out of the gorge. Thus, Manjusri was able to walk to the hill where he worshiped the Self-Born One,

The sanctity of Kathmandu's Pashupatinath Temple draws a group of itinerant ascetics known as sadhus *from the plains south of the Himalayas (**above**). This* sadhu *shows respect for the monarchy by wearing a picture of King Birendra on his headband (**right**).*

At the mid-summer's Gai Jatra, celebrants dress up both as demons and deities; a young man poses as Shiva with a pitchfork **(left)**, while the clay mask fashioned by a Thimi craftsman **(below)** represents Shiva in the terrifying manifestation of Bhairab.

Dealing with Demons

Demons have been harassing the good people of Nepal since the first settlers stumbled into the Kathmandu Valley. Down through centuries of legends, some of these evil fiends have been tricked into their own destruction; others vanquished by mighty sages. Still others put in a seasonal appearance only to be rebuffed by the goddess Durga.

But there are durable species of wraiths, ogres and others of their ilk that have managed to survive attempted exorcisms and purges and continue to plague the Valley and mountains with all manner of mischief. They tamper with the efficacy of ceremonies, curse the fertile fields with droughts and blights, orchestrate accidents in the home, especially in the doorways and kitchens, and haunt funeral ghats and crossroads, cemeteries and forests.

Certain seasonal demons that sneak into your digestive tract are believed to be responsible for causing indigestion and heartburn. Others drain you of the strength to work, and clog up your respiratory system with coughs, sneezes and sniffles.

Perhaps the most insidious creature of all is the kichikinni. It appears in the form of a beautiful woman. But beware; it's actually the man-hunting ghost of a deceased whore or nymphomaniac. The kichikinni can be identified by her long, drooping breasts and her feet — they are on backwards, heel in front, toes in back. She cannot speak but yelps like a monkey. She's notorious for luring men to her side in lonely places and sadistically tickling them to death. (Could that be where she gets her name?) Fortunately, the powers of the kichikinni are restricted to only a small area in her immediate vicinity. So if the man quickly gets back outside that perimeter, the last laugh's on her.

More powerful is the giant rakshasa. He's said to be able to devour a full-grown human in a single gulp. Fortunately, the rakshasa also has a weakness — a severe shortage of intelligence. According to the folk tales, anyone with an ounce of brains and a good heart can outwit the rakshasa and escape from its clutches unscathed.

Among the rarer breeds of demon are the mysterious mulkattas. Although these creatures are headless, they have eyes in their chests. An encounter with a mulkatta is an omen of imminent death. For those already dead, there's the betal. This devious demon inhabits corpses and can pose a threat to the living during visits to graveyards.

Invisible ghosts known as bhuts haunt the neighborhoods of the living, especially crossroads. To combat their malevolence, people construct sunken shrines dedicated to the grandmother goddess. When someone dies the garments worn at the moment of death are later deposited at the shrines; bhuts won't wear just any old or ordinary clothing.

In fact, Nepalese lore has it that every human after death becomes a form of ghost known as a pret. Rather than rushing off to heaven or hell, the souls of the deceased are believed to linger where they died and their jealousy of the living disturbs the atmosphere. Twelve days after a death, priests perform purification rites that permit the pret to become a soul again and be reborn in a new body.

More irritating than the common house pret is the pisach, the unhappy wandering soul of a person who died in an accident, suicide or other violent circumstance. In severe cases of pisach infestation, a priest must be called in to build a sacred fire and chant the mantra that pacifies the pisach. Otherwise, they ordinarily can be kept out of the house with iron nails driven into the thresholds. Outdoors, iron finger rings can keep the pisach at bay.

The monsoon seasons spawn yet another bevy of demons. On the night before the new moon, prudent housewives leave an offering of rice husks and buffalo entrails with a small votive wicker lamp to demonstrate their good intentions. The repast usually satisfies the appetites of the demons so that they refrain from further troublemaking. And if they don't, Durga slaughters them in October.

Swayambhu, and built a shrine. He located the root of the lotus at Gujeswori where he built another temple. Between the temples he constructed a city and introduced the Valley's renowned arts and crafts.

Contemporary geologists have validated at least one point in the traditional tale: the Kathmandu Valley was indeed a primeval lake eons ago. The Nepalese never doubted that. For centuries they have fertilized their fields with the rich black mud of the ancient lakebed, which must be mined despite the risks involved during the hot months of spring. But the system has worked well over time, aided by the indigenous genius for sculpting the land into terraces that make use of every square meter of arable soil. Food grows abundantly; thousands of farm families are relatively self-sufficient, independent of the cash economy.

Historians discount the rest of the myth, however. As far as they are concerned, the origins of the country are a mystery. The most they commit themselves to is confirming an invasion of Kiratas from eastern Nepal, possibly as long ago as 700 BC. Nine centuries later the Kiratas' stronghold collapsed before an equally-obscure group who introduced the caste system in which society was divided into four classes à la Aryan India.

The mists of prehistory begin to burn off around AD 300 with the arrival of the Lichhavis from North India. Extant inscriptions date from 464 and the records of Chinese emissaries from the 7th century. The Lichhavi kings are known to have been Hindus but they also patronized a local form of Buddhism that was already established in the Valley when they arrived, inaugurating the official tolerance of differing creeds that has been the hallmark of Nepal's religious history.

The Lichhavis also had formidable building skills. Even the Chinese were amazed by their palaces with their carved columns and gilded decorations. One of the most important cards held by the Lichhavis was their control of the trade route between India and Tibet. Legend has it that they solved any potential problems that might develop with their northern neighbor over trade or other matters by marrying off Princess Bhrikuti to Tibet's King Srongsan

*The eye-popping mask and costume of a performer are obviously of recent manufacture **(above)**, but their design and his dance steps date back to medieval times. A fearless group of Banepa children smile under a painting of the fierce Bhairab **(right)**.*

Gampo. Supposedly, she and his Chinese co-wife converted the king to the pacific tenets of Buddhism.

Except for a few stupas and statues, little survives of this glorious period in Nepal's early history. The reign of the Lichhavis ended in the 8th century and the Valley subsequently receded into a Dark Age. Various invaders established short-lived dynasties but hardly anyone recorded anything about them. Still, new cities like Kathmandu and Bhaktapur developed and new cults like Tantra and the worship of the Living Goddess Kumari took hold. Furthermore, periodic waves of artisan immigrants fleeing the Islamic invasions of North India enriched the Valley's arts.

Finally, the once-secluded valley itself was the target of burning and looting during this grim era. Raiders from the west and the south periodically sacked the Valley for a century. Then in the latter part of the 14th century a shrewd ex-princess named Devaladevi managed to pull the country's government back together; her hand-picked protege, Jayasthiti Malla, succeeded her when she died in 1366. Jayasthiti then outmaneuvered all rival pretenders to the throne. He was crowned King of Nepal in typically regal fashion in 1382.

Thus began the Malla Era. Its stability was bolstered by the suppression of the bandit chiefs and the codification of caste rules and regulations, a system since expanded and still basically intact among the Newars, the descendants of the Malla state.

During the long reign of Jayasthiti's grandson, Yakshya Malla (1428-82), other enduring characteristics commenced, most notably the royal patronage traditionally lavished on the construction of temples, palaces and public buildings. Yakshya also expanded the realm's boundaries and marked them with the Malla-style pagoda temples that still stand today at various sites beyond the Valley. But within a few years of his death, Kathmandu cut its ties with Bhaktapur and declared itself a sovereign state touching off turbulent times.

Patan followed suit. For nearly three centuries afterward, the three little kingdoms vied with each other and fought. They changed allies, captured satellite villages and seized traders routes, especially the one that led to Tibet.

*Using stone and vegetable colors, Nepalese painters have maintained a vibrant aesthetic tradition. Their subjects often include Tantric deities, like Chandamaharoshan (**left**) and Chakra Samvara (**above**), locked in steamy sexual embraces.*

The rivalry had more long-lasting consequences than petty warfare, however. Whichever kingdom controlled the routes north also controlled the lucrative silver coinage contracts with Tibet, which did not possess the technology to process its own heavy ingots. The contract helped finance a spate of building.

Under the Mallas the craftsmen were paid out of the state's taxes; the materials used were all from free local sources, except for the metallic embellishments like gilded roofs and bronze sculptures; the income from Tibetan coinage paid for that. If it didn't, the state simply adulterated the silver to raise the needed cash and erected the tiered pagoda, the bullet-shaped *shikara* or the reliquary mound — the *stupa* — simultaneously increasing the glory of heaven and the prestige of the state.

In addition to fine buildings and well-planned cities, the Mallas competed in cultural affairs. They inaugurated many of the great festivals held in Nepal. They also laid down rules and arranged for the payment of expenses by endowing *guthis* — associations with a permanent religious funtion — with land grants, many of which are still in effect. Temple maintenance was handled in the same manner.

The Mallas were highly-educated monarchs who composed multilingual dramas for performance both in the private splendor of the court and outdoors on the large stone platforms in the public squares. Entire neighborhoods were granted an endowment that paid for staging the shows regularly. Today the people of Byasi in Bhaktapur still tour their town every few years performing one of these music and costume spectaculars. Ironically, both the cast and their audiences hardly understand a word of the defunct dialects in which the ancient dramas were written.

By the 18th century, the prosperous Kathmandu Valley had begun attracting newcomers. They included resident Kashmiri traders and Indian pundits along with dedicated, intrepid, but utterly unsuccessful, Christian missionaries. The kings hired foreign mercenaries to staff permanent armies, a switch from earlier days when

*One of Nepal's renowned Gurkha soldiers is posted in front of a white-washed wall at Basantapur Palace during a festival (**right**). He wears the uniform and bears the arms traditionally used by his conquering ancestors before the British recruited them.*

they simply rang the great bell in Durbar Square to summon the caste leaders to provide fighters for the latest campaign. The three cities were harder to run but they were also richer — and that aroused the cupidity of such neighbors as the Gorkhalis of central Nepal.

Kathmandu citizens blamed the growing threat to the city's security on the libido of their king, Jayaprakash. According to the legends, he used to play dice with the goddess Taleju, the divine protectress of the city. One day Jayaprakash began lusting after her and Taleju split. She returned in a dream to warn him of his impending doom. Only by honoring her incarnation in the local Kumari could he postpone the end, she said. As a result, Jayaprakash instituted the Kumari Chariot Festival and began the custom of seeking the goddess' blessing annually to ensure Taleju's continuing mandate for his rule.

Despite Jayaprakash' divine intercessions, the Gorkhalis edged ever closer to Kathmandu as the year's passed. The Malla kings failed to perceive the danger inherent in their own disunity and their squabbling continued to undermine their future. Finally, on Kumari Jatra day, the troops of Prithvinarayan Shah marched into the city. Jayaprakash fled. His soldiers were too drunk to pull the chariot, let alone fight.

Following the easy conquest, everyone hesitated except the conqueror. "Let the festival continue," he announced. Nonplus-

sed, Kumari placed her mark of blessing, the *tika,* on the forehead of the Shah king. He and his successors have maintained the custom since; the King now receives the *tika* after Kumari's last chariot ride annually. The rite has come to symbolize the social and religious unity of the Valley's two major communities.

A year after he seized Kathmandu, Prithvinarayan attacked Bhaktapur. Despite a brave fight, the town succumbed to a terrifying new range of weapons called guns. The victorious Prithvinarayan returned to Kathmandu and made it his capital. The Shah Era had begun.

During his long military campaign, Prithvinarayan recruited other hill folks in addition to his own Gorkhalis. Chief among them were Magars and Gurungs whose descendants still occupy the outlying vil-

The spires of the stupas at the Boudhanath Temple complex west of Kathmandu come alive with the staring eyes of the all-seeing Buddha **(above)**. Boudhanath is principally-venerated by the Tamangs, Gurungs and other Nepalese hill folk.

lages and nearby hills of the Kathmandu Valley. It was because of this multi-ethnic army, as well as his military achievements, that Prithvinarayan became known as the "Father of the Nation."

His successors expanded the fledgling country's boundaries north and east to Tibet in 1792, then west and south until their juggernaut was halted by the British in 1815. After that the country's borders were closed to all but a single British resident. He was provided with a house in an area that had a poor water supply on a plot that the local people believed was infested with demons. Although the victory earned the British the right to recruit Nepalese soldiers for their own use — the now world-famous Gurkha Brigades — they gained no more of an internal foothold than the lonely, powerless Residency.

With the threat of foreign aggression eliminated, the Kathmandu court turned inward and plunged into intrigue. Factional struggles climaxed in 1846, the year Jung Bahadur Rana engineered a massacre of all his opponents, staged a coup against the royal family, took them into protective custody, assumed all reins of state and divided the spoils with his relatives, beginning the Rana Era.

In 1850 Jung Bahadur Rana traveled to England, a country he toured with keen interest. When he returned to Kathmandu a year later, he made two major reforms. He drastically revised the criminal code and abolished barbarous customs like widow-burning and human sacrifices. He also inaugurated the upper class fad of building palatial European-style, neoclassical homes and wearing fancy Western dress. Other

Ranas followed his lead and built their own palaces, usually outside the city in the northeast suburbs, spawning the development of a network of roads and markets. Otherwise, there was little progress during the reign of the usurper or his successors. Ranas maneuvered against rival Ranas and the government became too mired in plot and counterplot to bother about the needs of its subjects. Isolated behind the country's natural communications barriers and politically introverted, the Ranas ignored the craving for revolutionary change that became rampant throughout Asia during their final decade of rule.

Rows of identical stone shrines flank the bank of the Bagmati opposite Pashupatinath (above), Nepal's most sacred temple. Dedicated to Lord Shiva, the Protector of Animals, Pashupatinah is a magnet for pilgrims, especially during festivals.

Pomp in Another Circumstance

When Jung Bahadur Rana left Kathmandu for a state visit to Great Britain in 1850 he had everything a Maharaja could want, except a home fit for an absolute dictator. After a round of friendly receptions in the homes of England's high-born and mighty, he returned to Nepal the following year with grandiose plans to fill that glaring void in his lifestyle; he would build a proper palace just like those he had seen in Britain.

Choosing a plot for his residence was easy. The Maharaja picked a pretty spot in Thapathali near the waters of the Bagmati. But when he outlined his construction plans, the architects discovered they faced certain problems, mainly that there was an utter lack of plaster, glass and other building materials in Nepal. A small matter, said the Maharaja, we'll get them from Europe. And they did.

Along with plaster for the cornices and pseudo-Corinthian columns of the neo-classical facade and the corrugated iron for the roofs, the Maharaja imported glass, both the ordinary kind and stained, for the doors and windows; crystal chandeliers to illuminate the long, high-ceilinged banquet halls; oil paints and cameras that would be used in the creation of the noble portraits to decorate the walls; and, Victorian clothing to wear at the grand receptions and functions that were held frequently.

As the palace began to rise, the Maharaja kept builders busy adding more wings to accommodate an ever-increasing flock of relatives and retainers. He kept four rooms open to the public, filling them with hunting trophies, Rana portraits and a hodgepodge of European souvenirs, all in splendid disarray. It took several hundred servants just to keep the place running smoothly. But it was awe-inspiring nonetheless, especially the facade.

Before long, other Ranas wanted a palace of their own and began imitating the style of the Maharaja's. Mansions sprang up everywhere, particularly in the suburbs where they rose, grandly but aloof, behind tall walls and sprawling gardens. The Rana style reached its apogee in 1901 with the construction of the sinfully-capacious Singha Durbar. It boasted 17 separate courtyards and 1700 rooms surrounded by a compound full of fountains and landscaped gardens. Meanwhile, roads were constructed to connect the

Powerful Rana familes favored the accouterments of European royalty; the high ceilings, neo-classical columns, and staircases **(left)** and fancy furniture and oil paintings **(below)** of their homes can still be seen at the Kaiser Mahal, now a national library.

Rana palaces with the cities and markets of the Valley, and a thriving business in service centers developed to cater to both the autocrats and their legions of servants.

Of course, a lot of money was needed to maintain the houses. The Ranas acquired it by bilking the citizens through various taxes and arrogating all the prime property for themselves. When the Rana Era collapsed in 1951, the palaces fell into decline. Cut off from free access to the state treasury, the Ranas discovered just how costly it was to keep up such places. Built primarily for the purpose of accommodating ostentatious feasts and parties, they had no plumbing or heating. Roofs began leaking, the plaster was cracking and glass broke constantly.

The Ranas soon began moving into more practical quarters. By ironic default, many of the old Rana homes were turned into government offices. Today, the Department of Roads occupies Babar Mahal. The Ministry of Education has taken over Kaiser Mahal and turned that mansion's collection of 35,000 books into a non-circulating library. Min Bhavan has become the campus of Patan Commercial College. Rabi Bhavan is leased by an American aid agency and Shanti Davan has gone through two metamorphoses; first as a hospital, then as a school. As for Singha Durbar, all but the main wing burned down during a lightning storm in 1973 but even that is big enough for use as the seat of the entire National Panchayat, Nepal's 140-member legislative assembly, which functions like a parliament.

The growth of tourism inspired a scheme to dust off a deteriorating Rana palace in Lazimpat and renovate it into a sparkling hotel. After a year of restoration work, the Shanker Hotel opened in 1965 with 23 rooms. It was later expanded in two stages to 94 rooms, all completely rebuilt and refurnished. The only reminder of the days of pomp is the banquet hall. It has a high, decorated ceiling, painted plaster reliefs of goddesses on the walls and cherubim over the windows, and an entrance door with a stained glass portrait of Joseph and Mary, a couple the Hindu Ranas undoubtedly failed to recognize. The only other remnant of the original palace is the hotel's facade. Everything else, like the Rana autocracy itself, was too dilapidated to preserve.

Widespread demonstrations against the Rana regime broke out in late 1950. King Tribhuvan, who like his predecessors had been merely a powerless figurehead, escaped the fetters long imposed on his family and fled to India. With the king as an ally, the populace of Nepal pushed harder and the 104-year-old Rana autocracy collapsed. The king returned to Kathmandu to a tumultuous welcome.

the state visit of Queen Elizabeth II by directing an even more ambitious campaign. The Balaju Industrial Estate, City Hall, the Royal Academy, Hotel Soaltee and the Exhibition Ground were among the additions to Kathmandu's landmarks. That same year the king also introduced the partyless *panchayat* system of government. The monarchical system, with some reforms was reconfirmed by popular referen-

The king reclaimed his crown and implemented immediate legal and political reforms. He also reopened Nepal's borders. Tourists only trickled in at first but numerous mountaineering expeditions foreshadowed the flood of foreign visitors that soon swamped the country.

Meanwhile, Nepal's leaders concentrated on development. When King Tribhuvan died, the 1955 Coronation Committee for King Mahendra organized the first major beautification program for Kathmandu since the relief program that was carried out after an earthquake in 1934. Seven years later, King Mahendra prepared for

Devotion to the King *takes the form of a clay doll, fashioned by a Thimi mask-maker* **(above.)** *The skills of Nepal's Gurkhas are so respected that brigades also serve in the Indian and British armies. Here, a brigade stands at attention during a ceremony* **(right).**

dum in 1980 under King Birendra, who had acceded to the throne in 1972.

Official pronouncements claim that national policy is formulated and implemented "under the active leadership of the Crown." That's an apt phrase considering the style of His Majesty King Birendra, certainly the most mobile monarch the nation has known. He's constantly on the go, making the rounds of nearby towns and remote hill districts, inspecting living conditions, and listening to pleas and grievances.

By the very nature of his role the king is more closely in touch with the common people than any politician. Nepal is the world's only official Hindu country, and in the Hindu order of things the sovereign is an incarnation of Vishnu; just as Vishnu is the Preserver of the Universe, Nepal's king is the Preserver of the Realm.

Religion remains a powerful force among the Tibetans, like this monk at a monastery **(left)**, and the Nepalese alike, who worship the Living Goddess Kumari. Two years after her goddess' tenure, Anita has readapted to the mundane routine of family life **(below)**.

The Private Life of an Ex-Goddess

In some respects Anita Shakya is just like any other 13-year-old girl of Kathmandu. She lives with her large family within a quadrangular compound in an old-fashioned brick and timber house with creaky stairs, low ceilings and tiny rooms. She wears a light blue uniform frock to school like her seventh grade classmates and joins them on the playground at recess. She does her lessons diligently in the 60-watt dimness of home and waits, somewhat anxiously, for the evaluations next day.

Teachers say Anita is doing well and readily answers questions in class though she's still too shy to pose them or to initiate conversations with her classmates. School either bored or perhaps baffled her last year but that's changing. Now she seems to have accustomed herself to it and pursues learning with a quiet enthusiasm unexpected for a girl who had never been permitted inside a classroom until just two years ago.

But there is something special about Anita, something that sets her apart. She possesses a striking degree of self-composure compared to the restless antics of others her age. And she walks with an almost regal air about her.

In fact, Anita used to be a goddess, the Living Goddess, Kumari. For seven years, Anita lived amid splendor in the Kumari House. She went out only to witness the great pujas and to ride three times through the city streets in the spectacular summer chariot festival of Indrajatra.

Back then, Anita was the incarnation of the goddess Taleju, the patroness of Nepal's royal family. In that capacity she received an annual visit from the King each year. His majesty came to her private, sacred quarters where she placed her tika blessing on his forehead granting him the authority to continue his reign the same way Taleju blessed Prithvinrayan Shah several centuries ago.

It all began nine years ago for Anita when the reigning Kumari reached puberty and her menstruation began, making retirement mandatory. After examining the birth charts of all the young Shakya girls, the royal priests came to inform Anita's family that their daughter was eligible for the honor. When Anita passed all the tests, she was immediately installed as Kumari.

Her family earned everyone's congratulations but lost a daughter. Anita no longer belonged to them. Instead, she was attended to by a different family that is permanently assigned to the role and grew up in the rituals and seclusion of Kumari House. For seven years she lived there separated from her natural family. She received devotees, divined their future and went for the periodic chariot and palanquin rides. When Anita too reached puberty and it all ended, she enjoyed one last feast at Kumari House, then returned home.

Naturally, Anita's family was glad to get her back. But the transition from the life of a goddess back to that of an ordinary little girl certainly took some adjustment. When Anita was Kumari, she was permitted to indulge in whatever food, drink, game or fancy she liked. Back home, she didn't eat like her siblings at first. Her tastes were still too particular and her mother dared not insist on it.

Anita wasn't very talkative either but that was understandable. Half the household was new to her, having been born after she departed. Now that she has gotten to know the newcomers better, she's begun to open up more, eager to share with her sisters all that normal sisters do.

Anita is vaguely aware that her future will be different from theirs. Traditionally, ex-Kumaris were not supposed to marry, but expected to live out their lives as spinsters on a pension provided by the state. Nowadays, they are permitted to wed but lingering superstitions that it is bad luck to marry a former goddess makes it difficult for them to find husbands.

Anita has some years ahead of her before she begins thinking about marriage, however. In the meantime, she's enjoying life with her family and the private adulation of her younger brothers and sisters. They don't use her given name. To them she's still a living goddess. They call her Kumari.

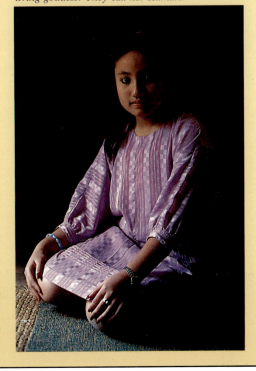

That the vast majority of the nation's populace still believes in the divinity of their revered king is readily apparent; excited throngs greet him wherever he goes. Ironically, modern helicopters and radios have played an important part in making this medieval institution the most widely accepted symbol of national unity.

In a show of mutual respect, the people return their monarch's visits, timing them,

as he does, to the season. In spring and summer Terai dwellers flock to the Valley to escape the south's heat, jamming tour buses that take them to Pashupatinath and other holy sites. In winter the mountain folk trek down out of the cold to do homage at Swayambhunath and Boudhanath. If a royal appearance or festival is scheduled, they mob the streets along with the Tamangs, Gurungs, Tibetans and Gorkhalis who live in the Valley.

The vast majority in any Kathmandu crowd, however, are Newars, the indigenous group that boasts of one of the oldest and most complex cultures in Asia. Newar

*The images of Nepal's royal couple are ubiquitous in Nepal. That their portraits rank a prominent place among paintings of Hindu deities (**left**) is indicative of the Nepalese belief that the King is the incarnation of Lord Vishnu, Preserver of the Universe.*

51

Nepal's colorful ethnic mosaic includes **(top left to right)** *a Newar farmer in typical Nepalese cap, a Tamang lady from the hills near the Valley, an old Bhaktapur farmer, a young Gurung woman and* **(bottom left to right)** *a Terai plains' farmer, Newar priest, Magar lady and a* sadhu *from the Terai.*

farmers were the ones who carved out the Valley's spectacular terraces; Newar artisans created the great temples and palaces that dominate tourist posters and brochures, as well as admirable sculptures in stone, metal and wood.

The Newars are tenaciously conservative. They cling to unique ancient customs like the cult of the Living Goddess Kumari, Tantric animal sacrifices, charming pre-

polite manner is another. All of the Valley's languages are well-stocked with honorific words; religion has cultivated subordination of the self and close living quarters have bred self-restraint. In fact, the Valley's ceremonial rites are often far less fascinating than the subtle glances, slight shifts of the head or blinks of the eyes that expand the meaning of conversations and reveal the participants' relationships.

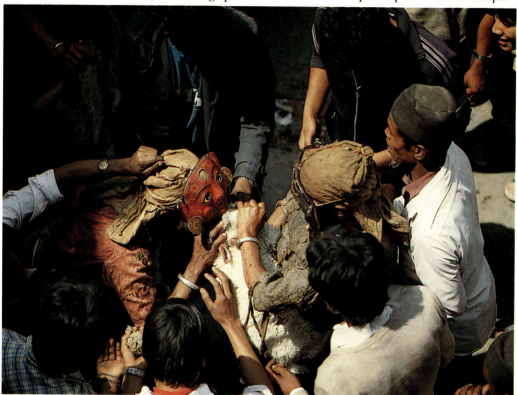

puberty rites of marriage of girls to immortal Vishnu (so they can avoid ever becoming widowed), and rites that celebrate old folks who reach the revered age of 77 years, seven months and seven days.

The Newars also display a peculiar passion for organization. They have divided themselve into 84 subcastes, excluding warriors, and a host of work teams, caste and neighborhood *guthis,* and such modern associations as political factions and the endlessly changing ad hoc committees of development programs and official functions.

The love of ceremony is one Newar trait shared by all the Nepalese of the Valley. A

Strange blood rites *in the name of religion still persist in the Kathmandu Valley. In a gruesome display of his faith, a masked Devi dancer drinks blood from the slit throat of a sacrificial goat before it dies in a slow and painful manner* **(above)**.

Religion and culture shape other facets of the Nepalese character. The collective nature of work teams and caste/kin activities account for the peoples' vaunted sociability. Rare indeed is the lone wolf. The attachments cemented during the formative years of the Nepalese usually last a lifetime; loyalty is a trait as common between friends as it is between a Gurkha trooper and his officer. The network of relationships in the Valley forms a universal insurance system.

A sense of responsibility is also inculcated at an early age. That's why visitors see so many 3-year-olds constantly perched on the backs of 8-year-olds; the older children care for their young brothers and sisters while their parents work all day long in the fields.

It's partly this social security and partly

the fact that the Valley itself is so safe from war, famine and extremes of climate that make the Nepalese so easy-going and friendly. For the majority, however, life is not such hard work after all, except perhaps for planting and harvesting, and friends help out with that.

The pace of the Valley is relaxed. If something can't be done today, there's always tomorrow or the day after so there's no reason to worry or get upset. Gorkhali neighbors may quarrel bitterly but an intermediary eventually solves everything; after that they wind up trying to out-apologize each other. Excited Newars bluster and threaten one another — until a mutual friend steps in and separates them before the dispute escalates into fisticuffs. In fact, the Newar language has a verb that means "to intervene between two people about to fight;" even belligerents expect someone to separate them.

These traits carry over into the Nepalese' relationships with the foreign visitors who have been flocking in and out of the country like migratory birds for the past two decades. Nepal has never been occupied or colonized by a Western power so its people have never developed a feeling of inferiority to Westerners.

The people of Nepal were exposed to literally dozens of varities of foreigners all at once so it's little wonder they found them a rather curious lot. But once they realized that people were traveling thousands of miles because they were enthralled by the landscapes and their own cultures, it came as a great boost to national pride; it gave the Nepalese something to discuss with their guests. After that realization, they wanted

to learn everything they could from foreign visitors, from their opinions of Nepal to their insights on the countries they came from. Even illiterate farmers became curious. Do you eat rice in your country? Do you have the same moon? The number of questions put to visitors is almost as endless as their content.

The Nepalese view foreigners as a peculiar breed who appear to have their own bewildering array of subcastes. There are group tourists, shepherded by in fast-moving flocks, snapping pictures on the run. No one pays much attention to them, except trinket peddlers and child beggars,

The ritual slaying of goats and chickens occurs every Tuesday and Saturday at the shrine of the feared Dakshinkali, the Black Goddess of the south (above). Legend says that she appeared to a 14th century king and commanded him to build the shrine.

but everyone gawks and laughs at the plump matron in the made-in-Bangkok miniskirt and the bare-chested sunburned chap wearing swimming trunks, dark glasses and Nepali cap who has three cameras dangling from his neck.

More serious travelers usually move about in smaller numbers at a slower pace, but are more shy of the local people than vice versa. Then there are the trekkers and climbers who come wearing big shoes and backpacks. They are too anxious to hit the mountain trails to tarry for long in the city but they pepper service personnel with questions in the hotels, bars and shops. Diplomats and international agency employees zip by in automobiles to suburban homes oddly similar to the ones they left behind in their countries.

The Nepalese find that the most accessible visitors are students who come to the Valley for extended stays and who plunge as deeply into the local society as possible, and the expatriates who have been so seduced by the Valley's charms that they have carved a niche for themselves in teaching, the handicrafts business or the burgeoning travel trade.

By far the most unusual group of itinerants have been the hippies, dropouts and "freaks" who began arriving in the late 1960s in search of some universal truth they couldn't find in their own societies: religious zealots who adopted the garb and rituals of some of the local sects; the classic

*Wearing an elaborate necklace of beads and pendants that includes a photograph of His Majesty King Birendra, an old Tibetan woman in Boudhanath spins a prayer on a "prayer-wheel" to heaven (**above**) in an ancient, time-honored manner.*

guitar-strumming, laid-back, unkempt, half-dressed, wandering "citizens of the world;" mad painters and splenetic poets; the humble Dane intent on imitating the Tibetans and prostrating himself at all the major *stupas;* the scruffy but intense, soft-spoken German who wants to set up a color meditation course; and, the jaded, veteran traveler in the pie shop exchanging mean comments on life's significance with an unemployed Nepalese youth.

Ultimately, the Valley is where the exotic meets the exotic. After all, tourism does imply cultural exchange. So for every Nepali girl in blue jeans and Western make-up, there's a Western woman wearing a saree and a *tika* mark on her forehead. For every fashionable young Manangi in his made-in-Hong Kong pants and leather jacket zipping about on a motorbike, there's an itinerant European in matted hair, holy beads and dhoti, strolling barefoot through town and country. Nepalese punk-rockers experiment with the safety pin look; women travelers pierce their noses and perforate their ears to accommodate Valley jewelry. The Nepali lady wears an expensive Swiss wristwatch, the Western man a Tibetan rosary.

Cultural exchange extends to cuisine, too. The traveler samples ordinary fare — rice, lentils, and vegetables — progresses to meat, dumplings, spicy chicken curries and *kebabs*, samples the sweets he sees cooked at the curbside, and accepts an invitation to a festival dinner. Then he tries the beaten rice flakes of a typical feast, along with pickles, roasted soybeans, spiced vegetables and meat dishes smothered in chili, ginger, onion, coriander and cumin, leaving a tang on the tongue that's soothed by a dessert of sweet curd.

His Nepalese friend, meanwhile, tries packaged noodles, bread, cheese and other homemade, foreign-styled food, advances to croissants, pizzas and ice cream, then graduates to a full, hearty Western meal, bereft of rice. For drinks, foreigners experiment with semi-sweet rice beer or the potent spirit, *rakshi*, which creeps up suddenly on you but does not induce a hangover. The native on the other hand eschews the home brew in favor of hops beer and Johnny Walker Black.

Tourism alone does not account for Nepal's headlong rush toward the modern world and ways. About 50,000 Nepalese journey abroad each year. Nearly half visit Bangkok, a lively conduit for Western dress, gadgetry, architecture and other notions. They may have heard about it in Nepal, but they experience it abroad and often return home with altered perceptions; suddenly they are inclined to rate comfort above custom, to put more importance on acquisitions and ambitions then on traditional relationships and recurrent events.

But for those who never travel outside Nepal and are bound to the timeless cultivation of the soil, modernization still means little. Their relationships still involve uncles instead of some unrelated boss, work teams and caste-kin groups like *guthis* instead of unions and committees run by strangers — unless, of course, some local genius figures out a way to mechanize terrace farming in the future.

All in all, even the most modernized of Nepal's people are a long way from abandoning their past. They build themselves new concrete houses — but only after a proper demon-busting *pujas*. They gyrate to rock-and-roll at wedding parties — but the match was arranged by the elders according to caste and astrological charts. They use modern conventions to accomplish traditional ends — motorcycles are

conscripted for the annual ancient New Year's parade and electric lighting and microphones enhance the street performances of contemporary satirical skits put up for the age-old Cow Festival.

In the Kathmandu Valley, the medieval and modern coexist — restlessly. Expectations of change rise like new hotels but fall as fast as profits in the off-season. And tradition persists, oblivious to the changing times, as solid as the sacred stones enshrined across the Valley, to which the Nepalese turn for succour and strength and visitors look to for new wisdom, or simply for inspiration.

The parents of Nepal shower their children with affection; like parents everywhere they have their own remedies to ensure their youngsters' health. For instance, as an antidote to dry skin, mothers massage their babies with mustard oil **(above)**.

Carpets for Dharma: The Tibetans

The most obvious characteristic of the large number of Tibetans who live in the Kathmandu Valley is their religious devotion. Every day in every kind of weather, in the early morning and again at dusk, they make their ritual circumambulations of Swayambhu Hill and the Boudhanath stupa. Young and old, monks and laymen, rich and poor, make their rounds, alone or in groups, in Western dress or traditional clothing. They steer left of the rocks chiseled with prayers, spin prayer-wheels which are either hand-held or mounted on the shrines, and finger rosaries to the soft cadence of mantras. They bow to their lamas, enroll their sons in monasteries, and wear the badges of their beloved Dalai Lama.

Indeed, Tibetans seem to be so wrapped up in religion that it usually comes as a surprise to discover just how business-minded they are. They are always poised to sell you jewelry, shoulder bags, trinkets and, above all, carpets.

Indeed, the merchandising of carpets has brought affluence to many Tibetans who once lived in poverty. Oddly enough, carpets were never much of a business back in Tibet. That the craft took hold in Kathmandu is the story of how an age-old devotion

The elaborate designs of carpets fashioned by the Tibetans of Nepal include elements of the fantastic and the natural associated with their homeland. For instance this carpet **(below)** incorporates a fire breathing dragon and a pheasant.

to a conservative religion has made a new business thrive, and vice versa.

In 1959 when the Dalai Lama fled to India, most Tibetans tried to follow him there. The Chinese sealed the border, but not before several thousand had slipped into Nepal and thousands more made it all the way to India.

The refugees left prepared to start new lives, bringing their livestock and all the property they could carry. Unfortunately, the animals quickly grazed the mountain pastures bare and subsequently starved to death. Thus, most Tibetans wound up in Red Cross camps, selling off old jewelry and valuable paintings at whatever prices they could get just to buy food.

At this wobbly turn of the wheel, the Swiss stepped in and set up the Jawalakhel Refugee Center. Well aware the Tibetans would have to make a living somehow, they discovered a few carpet-weaving masters among their charges and attempted to tap their potential. Starting with this core group, the Swiss Agency for Technical Assistance expanded training and monitoring, bought up production and helped locate other foreign markets. Within a decade, carpet-weaving became the Valley's most lucrative handicraft. The Tibetans themselves took over after that, building the business into the third largest foreign exchange earner in Nepal. At the same time, the Tibetans have earned the respect of their Nepalese hosts. It was Nepalese suppliers who provided them with materials on credit and their trust soon paid off. They found themselves receiving prompt regular repayments of their loans.

The trade in carpets has developed so fast that the Tibetans found there were not enough weavers among them to meet demand. So the Tibetans in turn have hired and trained Nepalese who were previously unemployed but who now comprise the majority of the weavers in the business.

Meanwhile, the Tibetan community has plowed a substantial portion of their profits into improving their own schools and monasteries. Both institutions have proven to be reputable guardians of the traditions of the old country. In fact, Tibetans have organized their lives so well in Nepal that it's hard to conceive of them as refugees anymore. They seem more like an immigrant group that has assimilated as successfully as the Buddhist and Hindu artisan groups that fled the medieval invasions of North India centuries ago.

Sadly, however, Nepal's Tibetans still are a people without a country. They carry refugee identification cards, those restrictive substitutes for the passports of an independent country. The border has been reopened and Tibetans freely travel between the two countries. But the refugees will not return to stay unless they are led by the Dalai Lama, and thus far he has resisted every Chinese blandishment. Even if the Chinese promised the Tibetans complete freedom to continue their lucrative carpet industry and keep the profits, a motherland that is subject to sudden shifts in religious policy is not an attractive alternative to their present situation. The freedom to practice their religion has always been the salient concern of Tibetans. After all, that's why they sought refuge in the tolerant Nepal kingdom in the first place. The carpet business has simply been a way of paying for their keep.

On a crisp early morning, *a group of porters chat while waiting for work at an intersection among the rabbit-like warren of lanes and melange of markets in the heart of downtown Kathmandu* ***(above).***

Back of the Book

This section provides a handy, compact package of exciting insights, entertaining tidbits, and invaluable tips that will help enhance your trip to the Kathmandu Valley. The main map depicts the Valley, some of its principal sights, districts and physical characteristics. Little-known facts about the Valley from items on its world-famous yeti to a unique tree that works better than Novocain are revealed in Valley Trivia. The sightseeing intineraries in Valley Tours are accompanied by numbered maps that will help you get around to some of the most interesting attractions on your own. For hardy travelers, there is a list of rugged, rural Treks and for even more ambitious sightseers a look at what can be found Off the Beaten Trek. Best Bets is a digest of the best of everything that can be found in the Valley, from nose piercing specialists to ice cream. Finally, the Travel Notes summarize the essential basic information needed to get you through the Valley and back.

*The elegant Bhairab Temple, home of the patron deity of Bhaktapur, rises in the city's central square **(left)**. The temple, which is more than three centuries old, is a specimen of the architectural genius of the Newars.*

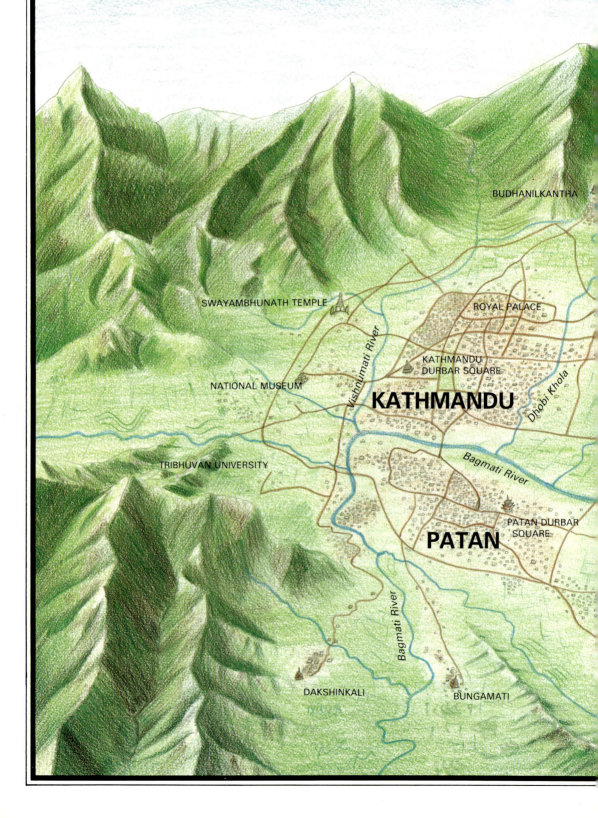

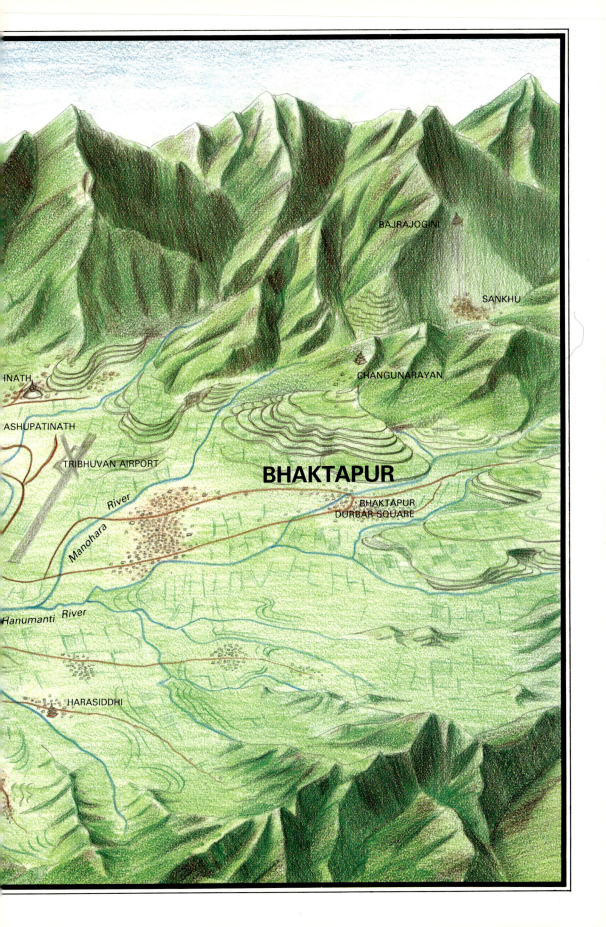

Valley Triva

THE SMILING SKELETON and its partner, the long-tongued, hairy creature called the *khyah*, which can be seen at various Devi shrines, are not demons; rather they are the Mother-Goddess' helpers. When personified in the Mahakali Dance Troupe show, the skeletons are played by children; the part of the *khyahs* are performed by energetic adolescents — in low comic relief.

THE YETI, the mythical "abominable snowman" of the Himalayas, has never been listed among the world's endangered species because it has never been captured and properly identified. In fact, it's been so long since any evidence of its existence has been reported that the creature may have eluded capture — by becoming extinct.

RANI POKHARI was built by Pratap Malla to console his queen for the death of their son. Once Pratap went there to bathe and was seduced by a demon that haunted the pond. The demon was eventually destroyed by a Tantric priest but the pond became a favorite suicide site. The Ranas curbed the practice by erecting the high iron fence that still encloses the pond today.

RITUAL CIVIL WAR was once an annual practice of sorts used to be practiced during the hot season when groups from the upper part of town battled those from the lower part. Rocks were the only weapon permitted, but the maimed losers were sacrificed to the Goddess Kankeswari. When Jayaprakash Malla tried to do away with the custom his subjects threatened to do away with him. The ritual battles were finally abolished by Jung Bahadur Rana after one event at which a rock struck one of his own guests — the British Resident.

FESTIVAL POLES erected for Bhaktapur's Bisket and Kathmandu's Indrajatra sometimes break when pulled down. To choose each new one priests lead a consecrated black goat to the forest and wait until it "points out" the right tree by butting or rubbing it. The priests promptly sacrifice the poor goat to the tree god, then cut down the tree. Devotees trim off the branches and haul it back to the city with fanfare almost as great as that of the festivals.

THE LAST LEOPARD ATTACK inside Bhaktapur occurred in 1976 near Durbar Square. Several people were clawed, but luckily no one was killed. The cat managed to get away.

MULTILINGUAL PRATAP MALLA, who wrote 17 plays in a variety of languages, immortalized his linguistic achievements with a 15-dialect inscription on the western outside wall of the Hanuman Dhoka Palace. See how many you recognize.

NEPALESE 'RICE PAPER' is not made from rice at all, but from the boiled barks of the high-altitude daphne bush. It is still used officially for all legal proceedings. A thicker, layered variety was used to make the religious and medicinal folding manuscripts of medieval times.

STAIRCASES in traditional Newar buildings must climb east, west or north. They never lead south because that is the direction of the dead. Thus, in order to enter the German-restored Pujahari Math first floor exhibition in Bhaktapur, you must walk to the end of the courtyard and reverse direction to go up the stairs — safely heading in a northerly direction.

INITIATIONS FOR SORCERESSES take place the night before the new moon at selected dark, secluded spots. Applicants are supposed to bring along a mesmerized son or husband as a sacrificial offering. Only then can they meet the old woman with the burning forefinger. After the blood rites, the aspiring sorceress will be instructed in all the magical black arts, including the forefinger trick. There have been no reports of recent applicants.

SUPERSTITION AND GOOD HEALTH merge in the dairyman's explanation for why he dilutes milk with water. "Otherwise the buffalo becomes very sad," he explains. Yet dieticians say buffalo milk is so rich that it is difficult to digest if taken without water. Similarly, when yeast is added to steamed rice and fermented to make the local version of beer, home-brewers throw in a chili and a chunk of charcoal "to keep the demons away." While the chili seems to have no readily-apparent effect, the charcoal absorbs gases during fermentation which would otherwise remain in the brew, then later enter your belly and cause some demonic belches.

ANIMAL SUPERSTITIONS are also rife in the Valley's folklore. Among the best:

— The cat hides its stool because he believes it to be a treasure.

— The tiger hates the cat for not teaching him how to climb trees and hide his stool.

— The rhinoceros makes sure it always excretes in the same place.

— The pheasant never goes to the Terai anymore because he was beaten up by resettled mountain people and is afraid to return.

— The mongoose divides the snake it catches into three parts, eats the middle, then rejoins the other two parts to revive the snake.

— When a cat has kittens it takes them to seven different houses.

— If a lizard urinates into your eyes, you will go blind. (So avoid putting lizards on your face.)

— When a snake bites a man, at first there is no poisonous effect because there is no poison in the fangs. Indeed, the snake regrets the attack so much he immediately begins to weep over the wound. Alas, his tears are poisonous. Unless a victim is bitten in water, which washes the tears away, they

will drop into the wound and cause death.

— When a dog and a bitch mate, they cannot be separated from one another until they have been seen by 108 pairs of eyes.

— A crow never dies unless it is killed.

THE TOOTHACHE TREE houses a small image of Vaisha Dev, the god who will cure the pain of dental work if the patient pounds a coin into the hunk of wood at Bangemuda Square, just south of the city's dentist offices.

THE POTENCY OF RAKSHI, the powerful rice-spirit known as *aylah* in Newari, can be tested by dipping a finger into it and lighting a match under the tip. If your finger quickly bursts into a flame that burns off the *rakshi*, you have got the good stuff. If it doesn't light, you have, in a manner of speaking, been burned. (Don't worry: You won't feel the flame or singe your skin.)

THE ENTERTAINMENT DURING GAI JATRA was an afterthought. The original festival was designed as a procession honoring all those who had died the previous year. It was initiated by Pratap Malla to console his grieving queen upon the death of their son. When she continued to cry, the king ordered the people to include entertainment, satire, and whatever else it took to make the queen smile again. The people responded with everything from song and dance to outrageous comedy, from the satirical to the salacious, that lampooned society from top to bottom. The queen laughed so much that the king made the fun a permanent feature of the procession. It still is today.

TATTOOS OF FLOWERS that decorate the ankles of Newar women farmers, and of deities and religious symbols on their forearms, were originally designed to cover their pale skin which was considered unaesthetic. Nowadays, tattooed women feel embarrassed by the stares of other Nepalese, but are consoled by the belief that when they die they can exchange their tattoos for food in Heaven.

RUDRAKSHA SEEDS from Nepal's elaeocarpus tree are holy for Shiva worshipers. Their value depends on the number of furrows, called "faces," on their surface. The rarest have a single furrow; the most common have five. Seeds of up to 21 faces have been found and tradition claims there can be as many as 32. Each type represents one or more deities in the Hindu pantheon. *Sadhus* and lay devotees wear long necklaces of the seeds around their necks in the belief that they possess many efficacious and healing qualities.

SALIGRAMS are striated, fossilized ammonite shells found in the Kali Gandaki region that are sacred to Shiva. The shells provide evidence that the Himalayan mountains, which formed when the Indian sub-continent smashed into the Asian landmass relatively recently in geological history, are younger than the rivers.

THE NATIONAL FLAG has a unique, double-pennant shape. The sun and moon symbols signify the solar and lunar dynasties that ruled during Nepal's mythical past.

THE NAME KATHMANDU is a corruption of Kasthamandap, the pagoda resthouse located just below Durbar Square. Until Prithvinarayan Shah officially adopted it as the name of his new capital, Kathmandu only referred to the southern portion of the city. The northern half was called Kantipur, the City of Beauty; while the entire city was commonly known by its Newari name, Ya. Similarly, Patan was once Lalitpur, the City of Arts, or Yala in Newari; and Bhaktapur, the City of Devotees, is called Bhadgaon by Gorkhalis and Khwopa by its Newar residents.

Best Bets

FLY TO MT. EVEREST just after sunrise with Royal Nepal Airlines (RNAC). The one hour round trip is just US$65. Check with the RNAC for details and departure times.

WHITEWATER RAFTING may be the Valley's greatest adventure excursion. Plunge into the torrents of Nepal's swift Himalayan rivers which cut through deep gorges leaving the snow peaks in your wake. Operators ply several routes and excursions last from a day's outing to nine days. Check with your travel or trekking agencies for details.

ART GALLERY. There are many but Indigo Art Gallery in Thamel, near the Chetrapati turnoff, is well-patronized by Western enthusiasts. Indigo specializes in stone-colored *thangkas* painted by the best of the Valley's traditional artists; subjects include reproductions of forgotten medieval masterpieces. They make unique souvenirs.

FABRICS can be found at Rainbow Handlooms at Tajamath in Bhaktapur's Dattatreya Square. Rainbow produces pure vegetable-dyed woolen and cotton shawls and furnishing fabrics. Original designs are handwoven with revived traditional techniques, unique and fast colors.

OM MANDALA MISO, SOLAR-DRIED TREKKERS' FOODS, and other great protein boosters are sold at Nepal Dairy in Thamel and the Supermarket in Tripureswor.

PASTRIES, ROLLS, ETC. are fresh from the oven at The German Bakery. Top them off with filtered coffee. Located in Jawalakhel, Lazimpat (opposite the French Embassy) and Chetrapati.

EXHIBITS BY THE VALLEY'S BEST contemporary artists are held at the Hotel Vajra in Bijeswori. The hotel features the work of a new artist each month.

FOR WOODCARVED PICTURE FRAMES and furniture of the highest quality in original adaptations of traditional motifs using classical techniques, call Lee at 411-141.

SOOTHING MASSAGE is best at Bina's. Take the Hotel Soaltee Road at Kalimati to the first lane past the hotel turnoff and follow the signs.

RARE AND USED BOOKS. The Order of Pilgrims' Bookshop in Thamel houses the most extensive collection, including a large number on the Himalayas and South Asia.

EAR AND NOSE PIERCING is done at the New Road jewelry shops. The shops use sterilized machinery, but be sure to wear only gold or silver afterwards to minimize the risk of infection.

GOLD AND SILVER JEWELRY. For a selection of unusual pieces, try Moti's in the house with the blue shutters behind Hotel Sugat in Basantapur.

METALLIC IMAGES AND VOTIVE OBJECTS are the specialty of Ratna Shakya in Patan's Mahaboudha compound. He is multilingual and quite willing to talk about the art.

BUDDHIST MEDITATION COURSES run regularly at Kopan Monastery, 3 kilometers north of Boudhanath. Call the Himalayan Yogi Insitute at 413-094 for schedules and arrangements.

TOURIST MAP. The Maha Map has the most detailed listing of shops and services.

THE NEWEST, MOST IMAGINATIVE jungle stay is the Machan Wildlife Resort at a secluded site in western Chitwan. Timber bungalows stand among undisturbed trees near a stream that has been widened into a swimming hole. In addition to the usual daytime jungle tours, the camp has a well-stocked library of books on the region, wildlife and culture videos, a small gym and yoga center. The resort can also arrange excursions to the hills where wild elephants roam. For more information and reservations, call or visit the office of the resort on Durbar Marg (Tel. 222-823).

ICE CREAM, for those who can't go for long without it, is available at Nirula's, Durbar Marg and New Road. Its menu includes some exotic local flavors that you won't find at Baskin-Robbins.

HAIR-STYLING and other coiffures are done by Thais at Omar's on the Hotel Soaltee Road in Kathmandu (Tel. 212-939).

DRY CLEANING. The Bandbox on Ganga Path,

opposite the Tourist Information Center, is reliable.

PHOTOGRAPHS AND WOODBLOCK PRINTS from the Print Shop Gallery, Thamel. If you're one of those who always fail to bring back a decent picture, you'll find a great selection here. Prints can be purchased from the collections of the Valley's top working photographers.

BLACK-AND-WHITE FILM PROCESSING and printing at Ganesh Photo, Bhimsenthan, halfway to the bridge from Durbar Square. Ganesh also has a fascinating collection of rare historical negatives; bargain for prints of Jung Bahadur Rana, extinct palaces, royalty, lively major festivals pre-earthquake Kathmandu, and more.

COLOR SLIDE E-6 PROCESSING at Raj Photo, Makhantole, north of Taleju Temple.

ASTROLOGICAL CHARTS are drawn up by Indu, a multilingual astrologer versed in the lore of East and West. Call 213-623 for an appointment.

MODERN FASHIONS are made with local materials by the designer, Shakun, at Wheels Boutique, Durbar Marg.

BRASS is the exquisite metalware of eastern Nepal. Chainpur Brass at the top of Durbar Marg stocks ritual vessels and pitcher, ornate cups, and "singing" bowls.

NEPALI CULTURE IN DOLLS crafted by Kirin Maskey of Bhimsenthan. These beautiful creations are arranged in ensemble scenes of local life including weddings and field work. Call 214-545 mornings or evenings for an appointment.

A WIDE VARIETY OF CARPETS are sold at numerous shops in and around the Jawalakhel Refugee Center, between the bus stand and the Ring Road. Bargaining is the rule.

PALM READINGS. There's never a dull session when Indian palmist Lalji looks at your lines. His place is near the top of Durbar Marg.

FREE NEPALI LANGUAGE LESSONS from Educational Training Services, Pulchowk in Patan. For arrangements call 522-912.

SPECIALIZED TOURS for individuals and small groups interested in more than the cursory visit of the country's attractions can be arranged by Thomas Silzer and partner through Yeti Travels on Durbar Marg. The usual adventures like rafting and trekking are enhanced by a staff of resident specialists in various fields like religion, history, archaeology, and ethnic cultures.

FOLK DANCES are held from 7 to 8 nightly at the Hotel Shanker after drinks in the garden.

BHAKTAPUR NIGHT AT HOTEL SHANGRILA is held every Friday. The entertainment includes the Mahakali Masked Dance troupe, the most spectacular in town, performing in a wicker lamp-lit garden. The food typifies that of a great Newar feast.

TENNIS, ANYONE? Or perhaps squash? Courts for either sport are located in Battispatuli, just south of the Pashupatinah turnoff. Call Murari Rana at 212-608 for information on reservations and rented equipment.

WOOD-CARVED FURNITURE, with traditional motifs on tables, beds, chests, lampstands, and other pieces can be purchased from the carvers' cooperative in Tajamath, Dattareya, Square, Bhaktapur. You can visit the workshop in the compound, which employs veteran artisans who worked on many of the restoration projects.

TAILOR FOR WESTERN or Nepali-style clothing. Try Dharma Ratna Bajracharya, Kumari Pati, Jawalakhel. Nepalese musical instruments from the small unmarked shop next door to the Mona Lisa at the top of Jochhe tole (Freak Street). There is another shop near the Chhetrapati junction. A variety of local drums are available from a shop on Yetkha tole, south of Nardevi Temple.

SHIPPING AGENTS with reliable reputations include: Atlas, on Durbar Marg, Tel. 212-402; Sharmason's on Kanti Path, 212-709; and, Universal, Durbar Marg, 214-195.

BHUTANESE TEXTILES, including intricately-patterned antique weavings, from Zambala in Thamel, 216-007.

NEPALESE SCENERY PAINTINGS in various sizes from Park Gallery, Pulchow, Patan, 522-307. It's also the best place for framing and dry-mounting pictures.

TIBETAN-STYLED THANGKAS, old and new, high-quality work from: Lovely Thangka Center, Durbar Square, Bhaktapur; Everest Thangka, Thamel; Dawa Arts, Dev Arcade, Durbar Marg.

HOUSEHOLD FABRIC FURNISHINGS, from Nepal Women's Organization, Pulchowk, Patan, 521-904. They specialize in block-printed table cloths, napkins, bed covers, pillow cases and many kinds of colorful doll clothes.

PASHMINA ARTS FACTORY in Gyaneshwar, near the Bangladesh Embassy, for a view of weaving the finest quality woolen shawls. The wool comes from the throat hair of Himalayan goats and is collected from rocks and bushes where the goats scratch themselves. Soft, light and warm, pashmina comes in several natural shades (pure white is the most expensive) and is also dyed, though with chemical colors.

LAXMI WOODCRAFT, 2/614 Bansbari, 50 meters north of the Ring Road junction, right side, is the place to get handmade buttons, crochet needles, chopsticks, chess pieces, etc.

PEDIATRICIAN, most recommended by Western residents, is Basanta Lal Shrestha in Chhetrapati. Call 220-432 for an appointment.

Small shops in Kathmandu *usually occupy the ground floor of an owner's residence: a thangka proprietor displays a painting **(top left)**, a mother watches the kids and her textile shop simultaneously **(below left)**, a Nepalese Muslim beadmaker reads between customers **(above top)**, and a merchant offers a variety of household goods in his general store **(above bottom)**.*

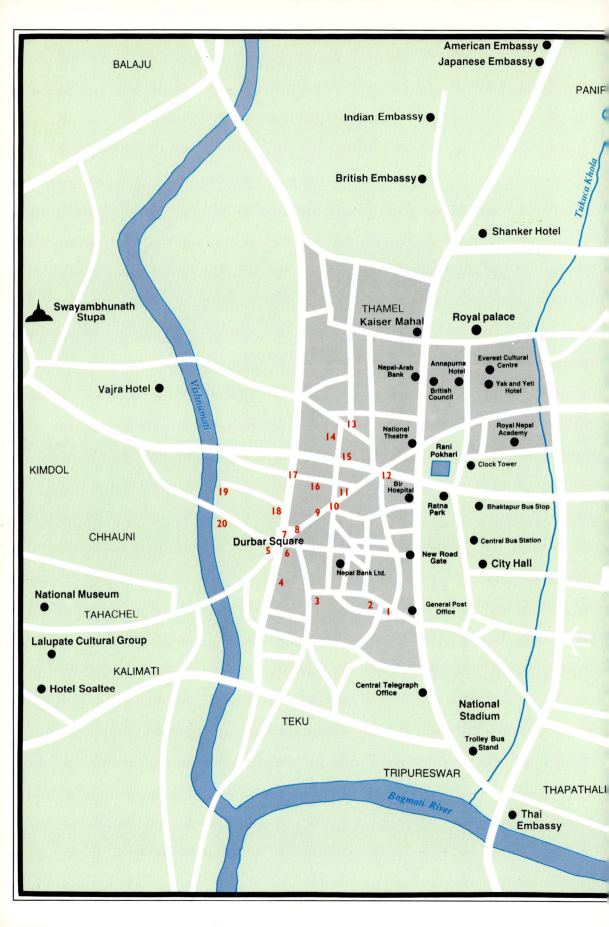

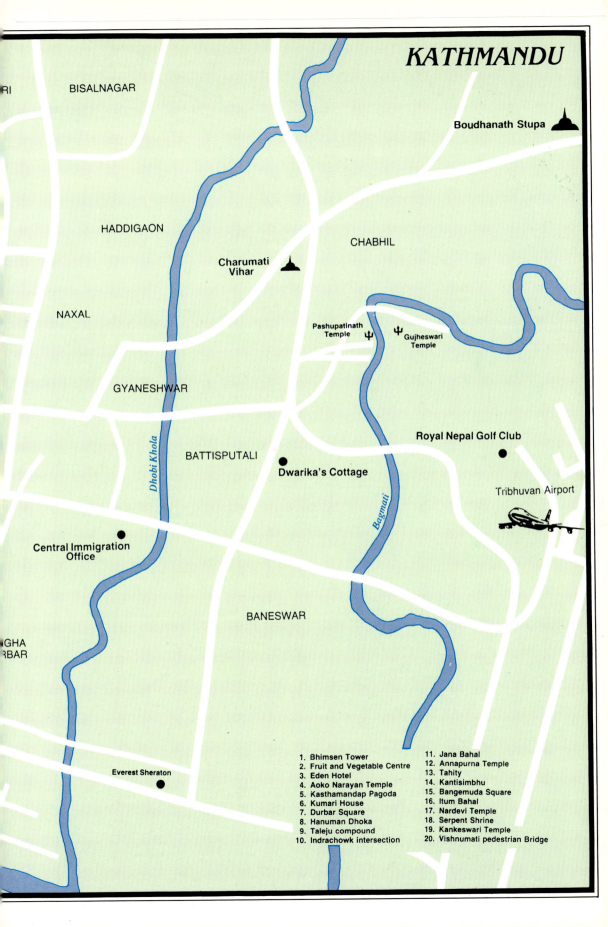

Valley Tours

KATHMANDU OLD TOWN. (Numbers refer to map on pages 72-73.) Begin at the **Bhimsen Tower (1)**, near the GPO, a 50-meter (165-foot) high monument originally erected by Bhimsen Thapa in 1833. Then plunge into the open-air market between the tower and the busy sunken baths with the gilded, crocodile-headed waterspouts. Food hawkers try to entice customers to their stalls with low-priced snacks and juices. Walk through the congestion, past the meat markets until you reach the **fruit and vegetable center (2)** on your left.

Browse through this vehicle-free zone to familiarize yourself with the season's offerings. Continue west past the next street, bear left past the white-domed shrine down to the **Eden Hotel** at the next junction **(3)** and turn right. You are now at **Jhochhe tole**, better known as Freak Street from its bygone days as the epicenter of international hippiedom. Some of its faded glory persists in the decor and merchandise of the shops. The **Basantapur Tower** of the old Royal Palace looms over the area's north exit.

Walk to the first intersection, turn left down the narrow alley one block to Chikamugal and right for a look at the **Adko Narayan Temple** compound **(4)**, an important Vishnu shrine, beside the motorcycle repair center. Walk north to the capacious **Kasthamandap Pagoda (5)** in the square. Erected in 1143 supposedly from the wood of a single tree, it has housed itinerant pilgrims for centuries. Inside is an image of the Yogi Gorakhnath, one of the most famous pilgrims of Hindu lore.

Swing left around the pagoda past the brightly-painted, three-eyed door to the **Maru Ganesh** *dyogah*, or god's house. Turn right and you arrive at the god's shrine, recognizable by its missing steeple. It was carried off to Bhaktapur in Malla times by an irate, dismissed priest. Maru Ganesh is the most popular deity in the city. He is worshiped before undertaking any journey and by long lines of devotees every Tuesday, Ganesh's sacred day. At the small rest house just beyond the shrine, devotional music enhances the evenings.

From here head east past the stone Garuda and three-tiered Vishnu Temple to the white-washed **Kumari House**, with its intricately-carved windows and doorways. Here resides the Living Goddess, the young girl who is never permitted to leave the premises except on some festival days. But she can occasionally be glimpsed at her balcony window. The inner courtyard walls with their wealth of fine carvings **(6)** are also worth examining.

Next explore the **Durbar Square** area **(7)**. Climb up the nine platforms of the three-tiered Shiva Temple for a panoramic view of the compound. The long, white colonnaded building opposite, the only post-Malla addition, was erected as a fortified palace by Prithvinarayan Shah. In the upper-story window of the brick pagoda temple on the north side of the square, figures of Shiva and Parvati look down on the action. Walk past the sacrificial post to the right of their temple, note Nepal's largest bell, above on the left, the huge pair of drums just beyond, and the decorated, upper-story window on the corner of the building on your right.

The mob of pigeons and the columned statue of Pratap Malla herald your arrival at **Hanuman Dhoka (8)**. Named after the nearly-formless, vermilion-daubed sculpture of Hanuman, the monkey king, at the entrance, the gate is elaborately-sculpted and brightly-painted with figures that include a Tantric Vishwarupa and Pratap himself. You can enter the courtyard and climb up into **Basantapur Tower** for a view of the city and, more impressively, of the gilded roofs and doors of the mighty **Taleju Temple** directly ahead. The courtyard is restricted to Hindus and closed on all but a few festival days.

When you exit Hanuman Dhoka, turn right to see Pratap's multilingual inscription on the wall 50 meters down the lane. The smaller temples in the area are worth examining for their variety of carvings. Facing north is the **Kal Bhairab statue,** a horrific, skull-garlanded black stone image unearthed during excavations at Nagarjung in Pratap's time. He had it shifted here and it became the custom to swear oaths before it. Supposedly, the god induced false swearers to vomit blood and die.

Behind the Taleju compound on your left, you'll see a stone **Garuda (9)**, the mythical bird-like creature, located near several mask and painting shops. Two small stone lions mark the entrance to the diagonal street of **Makhan tole**. There are a couple of tea shops in the lane to the right if you need refreshment and a breather at this point. Otherwise, walk one block to the **Indrachowk** intersection **(10)**. A brick and tile **Akash Bhairab Temple** stands to your left. Across the street, behind the front row of shops, is the colorful bead bazaar: Detour through it, then proceed to the market street. Shawls and rugs are draped from the temple steps. Shops

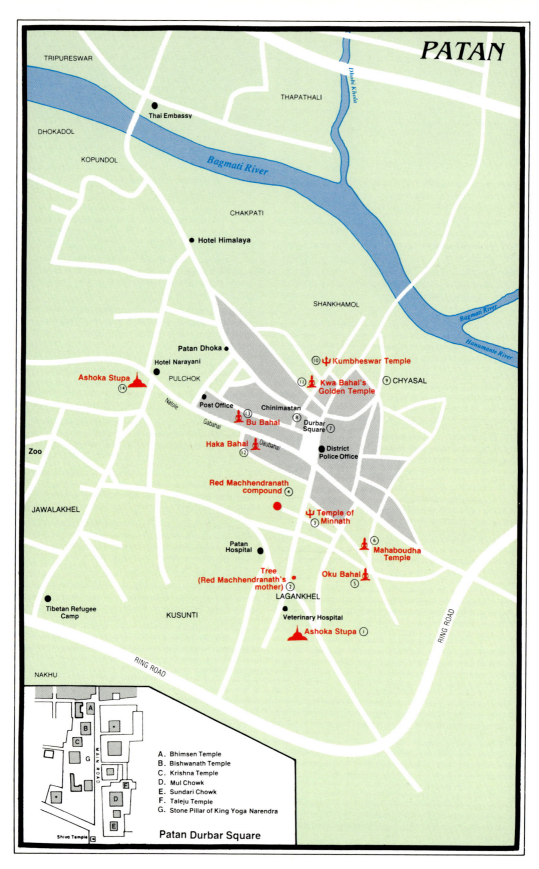

The next courtyard belongs to the **Degu Talle Temple**, once the Patan Mallas' personal deity. Back then it was the site of secret royal Tantric rites. Today it houses the weaving workshop and showroom of the Mahaguthi Shop which retails the handicrafts of the poor and the handicapped. Patan's own Golden Gate crowns the entrance to the last courtyard, inside which is a small museum full of interesting artifacts. (A, B, C)

Opposite the palace are several temples and a columned statue of the Malla king Siddinarsingh. And just before it is a Vishnu temple beside a platform used to stage masked dances in the autumn festivals. Flanking that is the fabulous **Krishna Mandir** which has Mughal-style towers; finely-chiseled scenes from the Indian epics circumvent its sides. A quick detour down the small lane just west of Krishna Mandir brings you to a small shrine honoring the headless goddess **Chinimastan (8)** where the walls are decorated with unusual frescoes: Above one doorway are four women, each raising a burning forefinger — the tell-tale mark of a committed witch. North of the Krishna Mandir two great stone elephants in front identify the Biswanath Temple, while the grander, three-tiered pagoda next door honors the merchants' favorite patron deity of all, Bhimsen.

Turn right here, then walk one block to a small, three-tiered Ganesh Temple and turn left. Follow the lane down to the water taps at **Chyasal (9)**. Compare the brightly-bedaubed Saraswati statue with the exquisite stone masterworks of the Lichhavi Era below it. Circle the tap and turn up the brick lane west two blocks, then turn right, passing the **Uma Maheshwar Temple** on your right, where you'll come to a concrete temple with columns and a dome at the junction. Turn left; 50 meters beyond is the five-tiered **Kumbheswar Temple (10)** which enshrines a four-faced Shiva lingam. This is Patan's oldest surviving compound; the temple dates to 1392. Excellent examples of the city's ancient art still exist in the vicinity.

Turn left and climb the slope 1½ blocks to the white lions guarding the entrance to **Kwa Bahal's Golden Temple (11)**, a 15-century Buddhist monastery. While marveling at the gilded splendors of the roof and deocrations, take a look at the ancient bronze statues in each corner of the courtyard; some are more than 1,000 years old. Exit through the back door into the adjoining

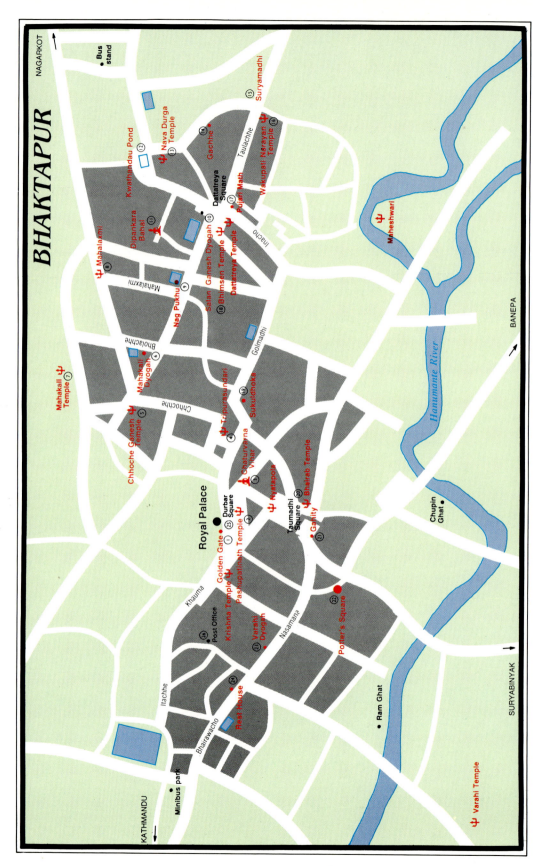

courtyard and follow the diagonal path to the next courtyard for a sample of the use of inner urban space. Then take a left through the doorway back into the street and turn left again. At the shrine with the three eyes, turn right and follow the lane until its end.

Make a right down the main street. Ahead, on your left, is the long wall of colorful **Haka Bahal (12)** where Patan's Kumari is displayed at certain festivals. Further down on the right, an arched gate that leads into **Bu Bahal (13)** features a two-tiered temple and a spacious courtyard that holds an array of votive shrines in different styles. There are more temples and bahals along this street that you will enjoy exploring if you are interested in the rich variety of Newar art.

The street terminates at Pulchowk's western **Ashoka Stupa (14)**. You can have a meal at the Copper Pot restaurant on this corner or at the Narayani Hotel just down the main road, or snack at the German Bakery two blocks south at the Jawalakhel Bus Stand. There are frequent buses and taxis that will take you to Kathmandu from either point.

MEDIEVAL BHAKTAPUR. (Numbers refer to map at left.) Begin at Durbar Square and the oldest of the Valley's three Taleju Temples. A gilded bronze statue of King Bhupatindra Malla kneels reverently on a pedestal opposite the **Golden Gate (1)**. The gilded copper masterpiece, considered by many to be the most beautifully-crafted gateway east of Florence, was installed by Ranjit Malla, the city's last king, in 1753. The multi-headed image over the entrance represents Taleju. Walk into the courtyard and around to the gateway to her temple compound. Entry is restricted to Hindus, but the carved, serpent-headed *torana* above the gate is worth seeing.

Next to the Golden Gate is the 55-window **Royal Palace**. The stone, *shikara*-style **Batsala Durga Temple** and the larger, pagoda-style **Pashupatinath Temple (2)** stand behind the king's statue. The latter is a replica of the one on the Bagmati, minus the gilding, and sports colorful erotica on its struts. Proceed past the sunken bath and turn right. Pass the shops and the pair of stone lions to the narrow lane on the right. About fifty meters down, duck to the right into the courtyard of the **Buddhist Chaturvarna Vihar (3)**, a monastery constructed to serve all four social classes.

Return to the square and turn right, pass the

white-domed temple on your left and take another right at the small Ganesh shrine. Follow the lane to **Tripurasundari (4)**, noting the "tree temple" beside the white cement building. At the Tripurasundari shrines turn left and walk north two blocks to the **Chhoche Ganesh Temple (5)**. Here the road left dips to give you a view across to Ganesh Himal and distant Manaslu.

After making a sharp right turn, follow the lane past old houses with carved windows to the even richer street of Bholachhe. Turn left and walk north, stopping to admire the **Mahakali** *dyogah* **(6)** with it gilded windows. The **goddess' shrine** is on a hillock **(7)** just outside the city limits at the end of this road. After passing the pond, make a right and walk one block east to the next mother-goddess shrine, to **Mahalaxmi (8)**. Nagarkot Road is the route east. Many of the city's farmers stream out to their fields in this direction around 9 a.m. and return at dusk.

At this point, turn right and walk to **Nag Pukhu (9)** where a stone serpent rises out of a pond surrounded by cotton threads, which are a different color everyday, drying on bamboo poles. This is the dyers' quarter. Follow the lane east to the next pond and turn left up the narrow lane beside the **Salan Ganesh** *dyogah* **(10)**. Go to the end of the lane, then left and into the courtyard flanked by **Dipankara Bahal (11)**. This Buddhist compound is the quarter of Bhaktapur's Kumari. The young girl is on display during October's Dasain.

Leave the courtyard and walk east to the end of the lane. Turn left, then right along the **Kwathandau pond (12)**. Round the corner to the **Nava Durga Temple (13)**, home of the Mother-goddesses and their masked dancers who perform throughout the city in winter and spring. Walk down the lane and turn left at the old houses of **Gachhe (14)**. Follow the lane as it swings around to the stupa and square at **Suryamahdhi (15)** and turn right. Have a look at the first compound on your left, the **Wakupati Narayan Temple (16)**; it's especially active on *ekadasi* (the 11th day of the moon) and on full moon nights. Continue west down Taulachhe tole, passing the Brahmayani *dyogah*, until you reach the east side of **Dattatreya Square (17)**.

The beautiful building on the south side of the square is the **Pujahari Math**, whose restoration marked the start of the Bhaktapur Development Project. The famous **Peacock Window** is on the western outside wall about 50 meters down the alley. Next examine the interior courtyard and newly-furnished woodcarving museum. Opposite the window on the north side of the square stands **Chikhanpha Math**, home to a bronze and brass museum that's also worth touring.

Next take a look at the **Dattatreya Temple**, the most active of the city's religious centers, erected by **Yakshya Malla**. The temple honors Brahma, Shiva and Vishnu combined, so it is active during virtually every festival. The buildings on the square are mostly *maths*, semi-religious houses endowed in the past to provide services for Dattatreya's pilgrims. All have been restored to pristine condition. **Tajamath** and **Dattu Math** also house woodcarving workshops where you can observe ancient skills at contemporary tasks. A **Bhimsen Temple** dominates the western end of the square **(18)**.

After turning left here, follow the main bazaar route. Pass several jewelers' shops, then veer west down Golmadhi tole to the old *math* at **Sukuldhoka (19)**, with its excellent windows. Fruit and vegetable stalls punctuate the route from here to **Taumadhi Square (20)**, the city's nexus. The three-story **Bhairab Temple** honors Bhaktapur's patron deity. But when Bhupatindra Malla addes the top two stories, a series of dreadful incidents occurred. Astrologers blamed Bhairab's envious consort and persuaded the king to erect the outstanding **Nyatapola Temple** to the goddess Siddhilaxmi. The five-tiered pagoda is the tallest in the land and was constructed so solidly that in the great 1934 earthquake only the top tier was loosened. Bhairab's temple by contrast crumbled to the ground. Each pair of carved figures on the steps represents ten times the strength of the pair below. You can admire the pagoda while lingering over a meal or refreshments in the **Nyatapola Café**, a converted medieval rest house full of carving including erotica on its eastern and southern struts.

Walk out the south end of Taumadhi and bear right to **Gahity (21)**. The street running down the slope to your left is the route the Bisket chariot takes in the April festival as is evident from the grooves on either side.

Continuing west, turn left at the first street and go down half a block. Turn right into the **potters' square (22)** where you can observe another timeless craft in the open air. Exit out the western end of the potters' square, then proceed up to the main road and turn left.

A block down you'll see the facade of the **Varahi** *dyogha* **(23)** on the right. The road then

dips to a multi-pillared **rest house (24)**, where you turn right and follow any of the brick lanes going up the hill to a main street and turn right.

Just before you reach the **Durbar Square Gate** you'll see an unusual 11-panel **balcony window (25)** on the right. Inside the gate, note the heavy stone Durga on your left and then take a few minutes to look at the decorative carvings of the **Krishna Temple (26)** on your right. The Art Gallery and the interior of the 55-Window Palace features a room with walls painted in the Mughal-like style of Malla era narrative paintings. Wind up your tour with refreshments at the balcony restaurant of the **Shiva Lodge** which is next to the Pashupatinath Temple.

For an even more enjoyable visit to Bhaktapur, stay overnight in the Durbar Square or Taumadhi lodge and attend a devotional music session at one of the temples or rest houses.

Points of interest outside the town's perimeter include:

A) Chupin Ghat, down the winding lane from Gahity **(21)** to the field, where the April Bisket Festival climaxes;

B) Hanuman Ghat, with stupas, shrines and the main cremation ground;

C) Maheshwari Ghat, an atmospheric shrine believed to be a popular haunt of witches;

(D) The fields beyond **Kamal Pokhari**, where you can watch farming (but don't be surprised if you're invited to lend a hand!); and, **Salaghari Forest**, west of the town past the military camp, a small wooded area from which you can descend to the highway, walk to the **Varahi Shrine** and return to town via **Mangal Tirtha Ghat (E)**.

Further afield, **Surya Binayak**, a Ganesh temple in the forest south of the trolley bus stand **(F)**, makes a great picnic or hiking area. The forest extends far enough for anyone to find a place of private repose. Early Tuesday mornings are the most active times at the temple.

Thimi, a satellite village of about 8,000, is three kilometers west of Bhaktapur. Take the trolley past two stops, climb up into the village, walk north on the main street and detour to wherever your interests lead you. Potters and dyers occupy the upper town, while mask makers have their shops on the northern link road, where you can catch an uncrowded bus back to center of Bhaktapur.

The hike to **Changu Narayan** begins from the unpaved road north of the **Mahakali Shrine (7)**. The viewpoint at **Naragkot**, a 2,000-meter (about 7,000 feet) hilltop northeast of Bhaktapur gives you a panorama from Everest to the Annapurnas. Buses leave every 90 minutes and take about that long to get there, including stops along the way. You can also hike to the viewpoint in three to four hours. Walk out the road a few kilometers to where a clearly-defined trail cuts down into the valley and leads to the steep ascent through the woods. There are several lodges at various vantage points in the area: Taragaon is the best furnished.

PASHUPATINATH. Located on the banks of the Bagmati River and dedicated to Lord Shiva, Protector of the Animals, Pashupatinath is the kingdom's most sacred shrine. Start at the **Gausala-Ring Road** intersection and walk downhill, between a flower garden on your left and a wooded slope on your right to the main temple area. A recently-erected, two-story **Bhubaneshwari Temple** marks the first junction. Continue to the next lane and turn right one block to the compound gate. Entrance is restricted to Hindus, but it is permissible to peek through the doorway at the massive gilded bull Nandi, Shiva's vehicle, and the silver-plated doors. Take a look, too, at all the religious paraphernalia on sale outside the gate. Then return to the first lane, make a left onto the next street and another left to the bridge and ghats.

Just before reaching the bridge, you'll see the **Devi Temple** with its unusual demonic figures painted on the walls and the erotic scenes carved on the struts. The stone statues enshrined opposite the temple date back more than one thousand years. Turn right down the steps to the ghats, where funerals are held and itinerant Indian *sadhus* reside. If you've always wanted to watch a Hindu cremation, this is the best place to see one. Otherwise, continue downriver to the large white-domed **Shiva Temple** near the sluice gate. Inside this compound stands a single-story, gilt-roofed pagoda temple to **Rajeshwari**, a form of the Mother-Goddess. The wooden struts, mounted above a row of gilded, smiling skulls, are carved and brightly-painted; besides erotica, there are domestic scenes including a carving of a woman giving birth in an unusual position — on her hands and knees. The most delightful scene depicts two craftsmen carving a wooden strut like the one they're carved on.

Cross the river here, bear left and walk back up to the bridge, temples and steps. Proceed right up the stairs to the end of a long row of identical shrines, then left up to the park benches above the bathing ghats. From here you can view

much of the temple compound and its activities. The river runs through a small gorge which some Nepalese say was cut through the stone by Manjusri, where there are two small meditation caves and a door said to be the gateway to Hell. Monkeys cavort in the woods and on the cliffs.

From the gorge, return to the stone staircase and climb up the hill to the *shikara*-style **Goraknath Temple** and the myriad neighboring Shiva shrines. East of this sprawls the forested **Mrigasthali**. There are a few temples, restricted to Hindus, and the woods extend nearly to the airport. Meander through them to take in the fresh arboreal scents and the sights and sounds of monkeys and songbirds in the trees and ravines. From the northern knoll, you'll get a good view to Boudhanath Stupa and the mountains beyond. Descend to the river via the same staircase; it passes by the **Gujheswari Temple**, again restricted to Hindus. According to some sects, the constantly-overflowing smaller well in the compound contains the sexual nectar of the Yogini goddess.

At the foot of the staircase turn left and follow the road to the bridge at **Gauri ghat**, where goddess Parvati once bathed. If you wish to go to Boudhanath from here, take the hairpin right path for a 20-minute walk to the stupa. If not, continue along the road back to the turnoff to **Pashupatinath Gate** and make a right up the cobbled path to the main road. Across the street there's a 17th-century pagoda temple to goddess **Jayabageshwari**, which has a Bhairab mural painted on the north wall. You are now at the edge of **Deopatan settlement**, once the ancient Lichhavi capital. Five minutes walk north takes you to the tall, yellow-spired **Chabahil Stupa**. Other Lichhavi *chaityas* stand in the courtyard. From here you can take a bus or taxi to Boudhanath or Kathmandu.

BOUDHANATH. The site of the Great Stupa, Boudhanath, lies on a plain five kilometers west of Kathmandu. Principally venerated by Tamangs, Gurungs and other Nepalese hill folk, the stupa has long attracted attention from Tibetans, who restored it in 1518. Tibetan lamas exercised limited jurisdiction over its premises from the 17th century to the mid-19th century. And it is Tibetan influence which dominates the architectural, commercial and social surroundings of this part of the Valley.

You enter through the gate by the road and circle it to the left. Just follow the devout, who'll be spinning the prayer wheels mounted in niches along the entire circumference. To climb up the platform to the mound itself, duck in the doorway on the north side, next to the shrine. Circle the dome for a view over the rooftops and descend the way you entered. A lane branches out here to beyond the north side of the compound. Follow it for a while.

Several Tibetan monasteries are sprinkled around the fields, and a new one seems to go up every couple of years. Here you can see monks at work, prayer or play and admire the wall paintings inside the temples. Backtrack to the stupa and continue your walk, pausing to examine the artifacts, carpets, gadgets, jewelry and clothing on sale in the shops and outdoor stalls that ring the stupa. A small lane to the left just before you reach the gate leads to a few *chang* houses, where adventurous drinkers can sample the local brew.

Boudhanath lures pilgrims, especially in winter when groups of Buddhist hill folk from all over the Himalayas, including Tibet, trek for weeks to get here. Their strange costumes color the local scene. They come for trade, as well as religion, and for a look at the capital, and many stay on through the mid-winter Losar festivities.

Among the Valley Nepalese, Boudhanath is sometimes known as Khasti, the Temple of Dewdrops, for tradition claims it was constructed during a 12-year drought. To obtain the water for bricks and mortar, the people laid out sheets overnight, rose early, gathered up the sheets and wrung out the dewdrops.

From Boudhanath, it is a short taxi or bus ride east to **Gokarna Forest Safari Park**, a royal deer sanctuary. You can tour the center of the park by elephant for Rs 100 per hour or horse for Rs 80 per hour, or ride a horse-drawn carriage around the perimeter for only Rs 30 per hour. There's also a small nine-hole golf course with clubs for rent. At the very least, walk the well-marked **Nature Trail** where you'll see herds of spotted deer nibbling grass and plants, a few stray barking deer, monkeys, peacocks, and the blackbuck antelope. The best viewing times are early in the morning or in the late afternoon.

POKHARA VALLEY. (Numbers refer to map at right.) For a serene view of the Himalayas, plan to spend a few days in the lush Pokhara Valley, 200 kilometers west of Kathmandu at the geographical center of the kingdom. It's about a six-hour bus ride from Kathmandu, including a meal break about half-way at Mugling, on a highway that rambles through the foothills and

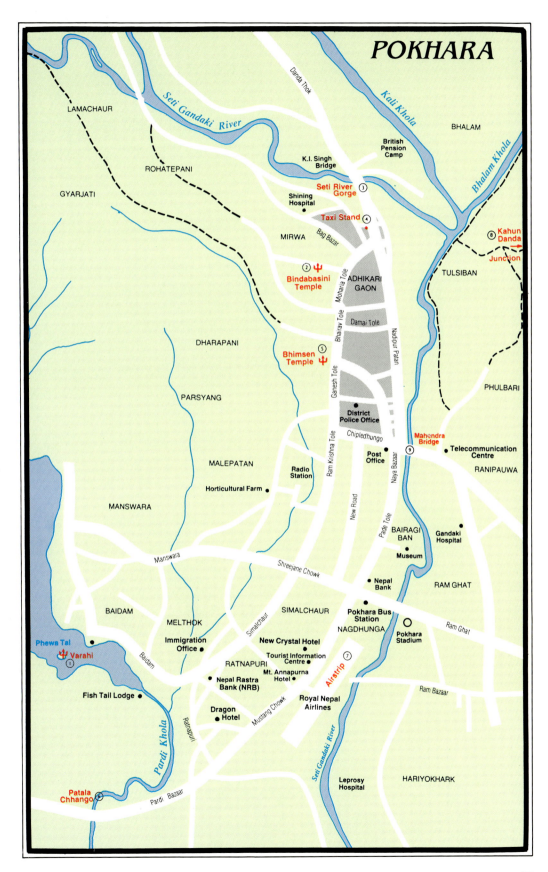

on a clear day offers a number of excellent views of the snow-covered peaks. You can also take one of two daily flights that provide a half-hour mountain spectacular from the air. There are a few good hotels near the airstrip, **Fishtail Lodge** and sundry small lodges along the lake, plus a few modest hotels in town. Restaurants of all kinds abound, but if you prefer to cook you can rent the equipment cheaply from one of the lakeside trekking shops and buy rice, bread, vegetables and fish in the markets. The Japanese-sponsored fish farm has reduced prices.

Nepal's second most popular destination, Pokhara Valley is an ideal mountain resort. At an average altitude of 900 meters (3,000 feet), it is always a few degrees warmer than Kathmandu and, with peaks of 7,000 meters or more rising just 30 kilometers away to the north, it's a better place for viewing the Himalayas. Some of these, most notably the majestic **Fishtail Mountain** (6,997 meters) are reflected on the surface of Phewa Tal, the lake southwest of the town that's the Valley's main attraction. The waters are usually quite placid in the morning, a good time for boating, fishing and swimming. Be advised, however, not to row out too far; it's hard to get back when a sudden squall kicks up. Pokhara Valley is one of the wettest places in the world, receiving 4,000 millimeters (157 inches) of rainfall annually. Some pours down in intense, if temporary, afternoon storms. Most boaters confine themselves to the lagoon between the dam at the eastern end and the pretty island temple to **Varahi (1)**, a short distance from the shore for safety's sake.

Pokhara town stretches several kilometers along a north-south axis. The popular **Bindabasini Temple (2)** on a pleasant site northwest of the bus depot is a popular starting point for treks. Visit it early in the morning when devotees are active. Then walk north and east through the bazaar to the **Seti River Gorge (3)**, a natural phenomenon typical of the Valley. Just before that, you'll pass the **shuttle taxi stand (4)** from where you can ride north to **Mahendra Cave**, the home of several hundred fruit bats, when you return from the gorge. The shuttle can take you as far as the **Bindabasini Temple**; from there it's a pleasant walk past small shops to the **Bhimsen Temple (5)**, where you head east to the bus stand for a bus or cab back to the lakeside.

Several excursions are possible from Pokhara. Thirteen kilometers east are two more sizeable lakes, **Begnas Tal** and **Rupa Tal**, nestle among low-lying hills on either side of the Pachbhaiya Ridge. A road that's passable by motor vehicle branches off the highway and ends at the shores of Begnas where tourist facilities are available.

The environs here are far more tranquil, if less spectacular, than those of Phewa Tal and the lakes well-stocked with the sportive, tasty **mahseer** fish. An hour's walk takes you to a spot where you can view the different colored lakes simultaneously. If you pack a lunch, you might opt to descend to Rupa Tal and if you take enough gear you can camp along the shore but be prepared to fight off mosquito swarms from April to October.

From Phewa Tal you can take a short hike south of the dam to see the waterfall at **Patala Chhango (6)** at a point just before that where the stream meets the Siddhartha Highway. For a longer hike, walk southeast of the **airstrip (7)** and follow the **Seti Gandaki** for about an hour to the natural bridge. There's a panorama of the Valley at **Nuwakot**, an old fortress 15 kilometers south of Phewa Tal, which can be reached by taxi or bus. Pony treks are available beginning from near the airstrip, but the sturdy animals are slow and uncomfortable for tall people.

Closer to Pokhara town, you can get another view of the surroundings by hiking to the tower atop **Kahu Danda (8)**, a 1,520 meter (5,000 feet) hill just east across the river. Start from **Mahendra Bridge (9)**, walk east one block to the driveable road that turns north. Follow the road to its end and continue on the well-worn trail up from there. It takes 2½ hours to reach the summit, so if you are going in the spring or early fall you must start before sunrise, otherwise the clouds well up and obscure the peaks before you reach the top. When descending, continue west at the junction halfway down **(10)** and take the alternate path straight to the river confluence. Then turn south and follow the Seti Gandaki River back to the bridge.

For good sunrise scenery, hike up to **Sarangkot** for an overnight stay, or further to **Naudanda** on the Jomosom route. You can go part way up a road by motor vehicle, or take the less-populated back route that starts at **Bindabasini Temple**. The first police checkpost is just outside Naudanda, about six hours trek from Pokhara so this is as far as you can go without a trekking permit.

Naudanda is perched on a ridge overlooking the **Yamdi Valley** and beyond to the 8000 meter Annapurnas and the majestic Fishtail Mountain. An impressive view of the latter can be yours from another angle if you take the one-day trek to **Burjung Khola**. Follow the Seti Gandaki past the Tibetan Refugee Camp and turn north with it. Burjung Khola lies on the east bank of the canyon. It's a great area for pastoral scenery, creeks and gorges, a hot spring an hour north at Bharbhare and an optional climb to a meadow at 4000 meters for a close-up of the Fishtail.

Treks

North of Kathmandu

LANGTANG AND GOSAINKUND. Langtang is a 1,710-square kilometer (660 square mile) national mountain park 30 kilometers north of Trisuli that can be combined with an excursion to the holy Lake Gosainkund which is 4,381 meters (14,373 feet) above sea level. The waters of Gosainkund are sacred to Shiva and lure hundreds of pilgrims for the full moon festival of August. Accommodations are sparse however, so take provisions.

Return via the Sing Gompa and trek north to Langtang Valley and the national park. The forested slopes are home to at least a thousand plant species, scores of birds and larger mammals like wild goats, black bears, leopards and yaks. The *gompa* at Kyangjin, the cheese factory at Yala, and herds of yaks are among the other attractions, as are the Langtangis themselves who are descendants of emigrants from the Tibetan border post of Kyirong. From Yala Peak, 4,900 meters (15,748 feet) up in the stratosphere, you can get a good view of the 7,245-meter (26,769 feet) Langtang Peak, 6,989-meter (22,390 feet) Dorje Lakpa and its slightly taller companion, the Great White Peak. The journey up and back requires about 12 days including three days for Gosainkund.

HELAMBU. The sherpas' other homeland, Helambu Valley, is a 3-day trek from the starting point at Sundarijal, northeast of Boudhanath. The settlements' average altitude is 2,500 meters and the snow peaks are only visible when you climb to the top of the ridges above the villages. There's a lovely forest above Tarke Ghyang, replete with colorful songbirds and small mammals. On a clear day make it a point to climb above the woodline to the vantage point at Yangri Danda. Each village has its *gompa*, the focus of cultural and social attention. You can return via Shermathang and the Indrawati River, take the road back to the highway and cach a bus to Dhulikhel or back to Kathmandu.

East of Kathmandu:

SOLO KHUMBU AND MT. EVEREST. The world's tallest mountain towers over the high-altitude homeland of the Sherpas, a region legendary for its friendly people, thriving monastic communities, sturdy porters, herds of yaks and the mysterious wildman variously known as the yeti and abominable snowman. Buses take trekkers to Jiri, from where it takes about one month on foot to travel to the Everest Base Camp and back. Alternatively, you can fly to Jiri; or further east to Phaphlu at the south end of Solo Khumbu; to Lukla, which puts you a week's walk from the base camp; or right up to Namche Bazaar, the biggest Sherpa settlement. The most important monastery is at Thyangboche, just north of Namche, and is set in the lap of Ama Dablam, one of the most beautifully-shaped of all mountains. It is here that monks keep the alleged skull of a yeti.

As this is the best known trek of all, accommodations are available in season all the way up to Lebuche. There's even a five-star hotel at Namche. And if you find the area too crowded, there are plenty of other excursions possible. Flight shedules are a problem, however; weather conditions often cause cancellations, especially of return flights.

ARUN VALLEY. This is a lesser-visited area in eastern Nepal that's especially great for anglers. It is accessible via Dhankuta or the airfield at Tumlingtar. The route north follows the Arun River to Mt. Makalu, 8,481 meters (27,825 feet). However, there is far less available in the way of accommodations and from Nun to the base camp there are neither shops nor lodges. The settled areas are inhabited by Rais and Limbus, believed to be descendants of the ancient Kiratas. Northwest of Tumlingtar, the town of Chainpur produces nationally-famous metal vessels, for ritual or daily use. Dhaka-style weaving is popular throughout the area and you can often see women outdoors at their looms, laying in the complex patterns for caps and shawls that are distributed throughout the country.

ILAM. In far eastern Nepal in the Mahabharats, Ilam is Nepal's tea-growing center. A road passable to motor vehicles branches north from the main highway to the town which is perched on a ridge carpeted with tea gardens on all sides. There are a few simple lodges and, if you've brought the gear, it's possible to trek north for a few days for good views of Kanchenjunga which at 8,598 meters (28,208 feet) is the world's third highest peak.

From Pokhara

ANNAPURNA SANCTUARY. One of the most majestic mountain views possible, this site is six days from Pokhara. Go via Birethanti, then north to the Gurung villages of Ghandrung and Chumra where you can pick up any extra gear you may need. The next night you sleep at Hinko Cave, and the following day arrive at the sanctuary in the glacier-cut cirque at the base of the Annapurnas. Besides the breathtaking scenery, you can view migrating birds like steppe eagles in early spring and late fall.

MUKTINATH. The Place of Deliverance, as it translates, is a temple sited at 3,798 meters (12,500 feet), north of Annapurna that is popular with both Nepalese and Indian pilgrims. A natural gas flame emitted from a rock fissure and a spring flowing into the courtyard through 108 carved spouts, add to the setting's magical aura.

It's an 8-day journey to Muktinath via Birethanti, Ghorepani, and the Kali Gandaki Canyon, a gaping gash between the massifs of Dhaulagiri and Annapurna. The scenery changes from jungled lowland and rhododendron forests to twisted evergreens and desert valleys where an 80-kilometer per hour wind blows from 10 a.m. to 4 a.m. daily.

The trek to Muktinath is flush with accommodations because the route follows the old Thakali-managed salt trail from Tibet. *Gompas*, isolated stupas, piles of prayer stones and fortified hill towns decorate the upper landscapes. Mule teams, Thakalis on horseback, and occasional yak herds ply the same trails as trekkers. There's an airstrip at Jomosom that has early morning flights back to Pokhara and Kathmandu, an experimental orchard at Marpha, a hot springs at Tatopani, and an option to return south of the latter through the Kali Gandaki to the paper-making villages opposite Baglung, then cut to the highway. Or you can return via Ghorepani, descend to Ghandrung and trek to the Annapurna Sanctuary.

MANANG AND THORONG PASS. Start at Dhumre, 70 kilometers east of Pokhara, and go north up the Marsyandi River Valley to the northern slopes of the Annapurnas. The route then turns west, passing cliffside villages and monasteries to the great *gompa* at Brega, which is more than 400 years old, and the major settlement of Manang. From Brega Hill, you'll have a splendid view of the Annapurnas looking south. You can also climb to a forested plateau at 4000 meters to see a gargantuan frozen waterfall. From Manang, it's possible for the hardier trekkers to take the route up to and over the Thorong Pass at 5,416 meters (17,769 feet), stopping overnight to acclimatize. After a gradual morning climb, cross and descend to Muktinath to take the route back to Pokhara and complete a 3-week circuit of the Annapurnas.

Further West

LAKE RARA. This is a remote beauty in western Nepal that must be approached from Jumla after a flight from Kathmandu. At 2,340 meters (7,677 feet) Jumla's temples and pillars testify to its past importance as a post of the medieval Khasa Kingdom, which reached its peak in the 14th century when it launched several raids on the distant Kathmandu Valley. From here it's four days to the 10-square kilometer lake set at 2,980 meters (9,777 feet) among forests and a 106-square kilometer (41 square mile) national park that is a favorite stopover for migratory birds.

Excursions

KAKANI, TRISULI, NAWAKOT. Kakani is a vantage point 29 kilometers northwest of Kathmandu on the Trisuli route, a 45-minute bus ride, then a half-hour walk to the edge of a ridge. There's a nice lodge here with a full view forward to Ganesh Himal (a triple-humped snow peak) and backward to the Kathmandu Valley. The river town of Trisuli, 42 kilometers further on, is the last major town before the trekking routes to Langtang and Gosainkund begin. There are several inexpensive lodges near the bridge. Here, you can see colorful mountain folk trading in the bazaars and you can also visit the Trisuli Dam, which generates hydroelectric power for Kathmandu. Next morning, cross the river and hike up to Nawakot, a medieval fortress which was used to guard the trade route to Tibet; when Prithvinarayan Shah captured Nawakot in 1744, he imposed an economic blockade on the Kathmandu Valley. Malla Era temples and buildings mark the site and there's a good view of mountains that are not visible from Trisuli.

GORKHA AND MANKAMNA. Gorkha, the capital of the Shah Dynasty from its establishment in 1559 until the conquest of Kathmandu in 1768, is located at an altitude of 1,143 meters (3,350 feet) halfway between Kathmandu and Pokhara, about an hour by bus from the highway junction at Khaireni. Alternatively, you can trek there in four days from either Pokhara or Trisuli. Mt. Manaslu, a giant at 8,156 meters (26,758 feet), towers north of the town, which hugs the southern slope of a ridge just above the winter fog line. The Bisauni Hotel offers moderate accommodations just below the bus stand, and there are more spartan quarters at several cheap trekkers' lodges. The town has a modest Durbar Square at one end, and a two-tier Shiva Temple. Gorkha's premier attraction, however, is the old Royal Palace, a half-hour hike uphill culminating in a long flight of chiseled stone steps. The palace was built by Newar artisans in red brick, wood and tile, with typical carved ornamentation. There's splendid views across to the mountains that continue as you hike east along the ridge. Energetic local pilgrims walk from here to Mankamna Temple, about a 6-hour journey. It's situated on the edge of a plateau 10 kilometers north of the highway. Because the goddess Mankamna is said to grant the suppliant any sincere wish, there are several simple lodges serving this popular Nepalese retreat. After making your wish in the morning, it's about five to six hours of walking to the highway at Mugling where you can have a meal and catch one of the buses back to Kathmandu, three hours away.

ROYAL CHITWAN NATIONAL PARK. For an adventurous plunge into a preserved wilderness of

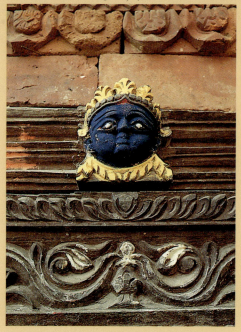

primeval Asia, try Chitwan. Sprawling over 932 square kilometers (360 square miles) of riverine jungle and small hills, Chitwan was once a royal hunting preserve in the Rana Era when the most exciting thing kings were permitted to do was to go on safari. More than 40 elusive tigers stalk the jungle, but the real star is the one-horned Indian Rhinoceros; about 50 inhabit the sanctuary and, because they snack during the day, are easy to observe. Three types of deer, wild boar, a plethora of birds of all songs and sizes and the narrow-snouted garial are also common. Deeper in the park lurk the leopard, the wild buffalo and the bison.

Chitwan lies 120 kilometers (75 miles) southwest of Kathmandu and can be reached by bus via Narayanghat. There are several camps just within and just outside the park perimeters. A typical itinerary consists of a guided afternoon walk through the jungle to look for deer and rhino, an early morning bird-watching jaunt, a river journey by dugout canoe to see garials and water birds and an elephant ride through the tall grass that will provide you with a safe, close-up view of the rhinos. Food, half-Western and half-local, is palatable, the sleeping quarters are comfortable and the guides savvy, polite and enthusiastic. River life makes for a diverting scene of busy dugouts, bathers and pack elephants in the mornings.

Much deeper within the park itself is Tiger Tops, Chitwan's best-organized, best-located camp. You pay more here but you go in style, flying to the airstrip at Meghauli where elephants parked at the airport provide limousine service, of a sort, to luxurious treetop bungalows. You can also opt for the well-furnished tented camp on the river an hour west, or stay in special quarters in a nearby Tharu village that features tribal dances as entertainment at night. Experienced naturalists will take you on safari by boat, elephant, jeep or on foot. Sightings of the tiger, normally a shy, solitary, nocturnal prowler, are frequent here. The best time to visit is November through January when the distant Himalayas make a frequent backdrop and the weather is slightly cool and refreshing. At an altitude of just 150 meters (492 feet), the area gets progressively hotter beginning in February and the park closes during the summer monsoon months.

ROYAL BARDIA NATIONAL PARK. Located way out in little-known western Nepal, Tiger Tops opened a tented camp here in 1984 on the banks of the Karnali River, 4½-hours drive from the airport at Nepalgang. At the foot of the Siwalik Hills, Bardia encompasses nearly 1000 square kilometers (386 square miles) of swamp, river, field and forest. Among its denizens are wild elephants, tigers, leopards, blackbucks, blue bulls, sloth bears, several types of deer, marsh muggers, fresh-water dolphins and garials. The waters are also well-stocked with fish, especially the tasty *mahseer*.

LUMBINI. Down in the Terai, 250 kilometers (156 miles) southwest of Kathmandu, is the birthplace of Lord Buddha, one of the primary pilgrimage sites for Buddhists from around the world. One ancient disciple was the ancient Indian Emperor Asoka, who erected an inscribed pillar to commemorate his visit in 250 BC. Only discovered in 1895, the pillar today stands beside a shrine to Mayadevi, the Buddha's mother, that marks the site where she gave birth. There are several ruins, an old Tibetan monastery, some modern shrines, and both luxury and simple accommodations in the neighborhood. To get there, take the bus 21 kilometers (13 miles) west of Bhairawa, the border town.

JANAKPUR. For Hindus, the most sacred Terai town is Janakpur, 128 kilometers (80 miles) southeast of Kathmandu. This ancient city is named after King Janaki, the father of the goddess Sita, wife of Rama and heroine of the epic *Ramayana*. A salmon pink marble temple in the 17th century Mughal style was erected to her here by an Indian *rani* in 1910. The layout and architecture of the entire town has an Indian atmosphere. As the capital of the classical Mithila state, the many water tanks, ghats, and temple and palace ruins in Janakpur reveals a fair measure of its ancient glory.

Off the Beaten Trek

KIRTIPUR AND VICINITY. Kirtipur is a rather neglected example of traditional Newar town situated astride a twin hillock 5 kilometers southwest of Kathmandu. The bus ride starts from Shahid Gate and ends just past the Tribhuvan University campus. From there it's a short walk up to the town. The eastern hillock, with its monastery and stupas, is largely Buddhist; the western, where most pagoda temples stand, mainly Hindu. The town's feature attraction is the Bagh Bhairab Temple which lies in the saddle between the hillocks. Built in pagoda style, the temple has a rectangular canopy with 13 gilded spires. Attached to the walls are some of the weapons surrendered when the town fell to the Gorkhalis of Prithvinarayan Shah. The stone statues of the Mother Goddesses mounted near the compound entrance are among the earliest ever made and to the right of the temple is an extraordinary birth-giving sculpture.

A half-hour hike east from Kirtipur takes you to Adinath Hill, skirted by a forest and surmounted by a Malla Era temple to Lokeswar, God of Compassion. Climb the stone staircase from the road, which takes you right to the entrance to a compound wryly known as "the pots and pans temple." You will find out why when you enter; an enormous variety of tools, vessels and utensils hang on the walls. The sanctum houses a red-faced idol, all but a twin to Patan's Red Machhendranath except for the eyes which look towards heaven.

Below Adinath Hill lies Chobar Gorge, the legendary spot where Manjusri slashed through the wall of rock that kept the Valley a lake. A suspension bridge imported from Scotland in 1903 straddles the chasm. On the western side are several caves where famous yogis of the past, such as Gorakhnath, are said to have gone to meditate. The ancient texts claim that the caves are connected by secret tunnels to an underground lake.

An interesting Ganesh Temple, Jal Binayak, is located just south of the gorge. It's a popular site for picnics and weddings and is reputed to be the place to pray for strength of character. Another kilometer down the road takes you to Taudah, a small but very deep pond that is traditionally regarded as the abode of the Nagaraja Karkatoa. His vast wealth is said to lie at the bottom of this pond. Rana autocrats tried to excavate this treasure but failed to reach the bottom.

THANKOT AND CHANDRAGIRI. The last town on the Tribhuvan Rajpath before leaving the Valley, Thankot sprawls along the hillside above the highway. In the main square stands the two-tiered Mahalaxmi Temple which has erotica carved on its struts. A path above the town climbs through the forest to the *chaitya* at the peak of Chandragiri, the "Mountain of the Moon." This sentinel of the southwest rises to 2,423 meters (7,950 feet). From the *chaitya* you can descend directly to Mata Tirtha, a large bathing tank with a small pool in which people say you can see the reflection of your mother's face. You can also hike east to the smaller summit of Champa Devi or walk down to Machhegaon, home of a small temple to Lord Vishnu's incarnation as a fish. From either terminus it's a half-hour walk back to the highway where you can catch a bus to Kathmandu.

PHARPING AND DAKSHINKALI. South of Chobar the road extends beyond the geographical limits of the Valley, passing Pharping before terminating at Dakshinkali. Pharping is a small village noted for both local and Tibetan shrines. Near the entrance to the village lies the Sekh Narayan Temple, flanking two water tanks. In the village center stands a taller temple to Bhimsen. A stone staircase rises along the hillside just above the village to the 17th century temple to Vajrajogini, an important goddess in the Tantric pantheon. Higher up is a small shrine to Ganesh, and above that a cave which the Hindus named after the yogi Gorakhnath, whose handprint and footprints are embedded in the ground in front. Tibetans revere it as Asura Cave, after the demon that was reputed to have been subjugated here by Guru Padmasambhava during a retreat he made in preparation for his journey across the Himalayas. Besides building a monastery here, they have adorned the vicinity with colorful prayer flags. Stand back and use them as a frame for the splendid view across the Valley.

Twenty kilometers from Kathmandu the road ends at a popular shrine to Dakshinkali, the Black Goddess of the south who appeared to a 14th century king and commanded him to build her this shrine. Lying in a nook of the woods by a confluence, Dakshinkali makes a pleasant picnic site, though the action at the black stone image of the goddess may not be to everyone's taste. Every Tuesday and Saturday, worshipers slaughter dozens of goats, buffaloes and chickens as a sacrifice aimed at slaking the blood thirst of Kali. Devotees who don't care for the gore often prefer to climb the path that winds behind and above to the smaller shrine atop a hillock which houses Dakshinkali's mother.

KOKONAH AND BUNGAMATI. These twin villages, established in the 16th century, lie at the end of the southwest radial road from the Ring Road south of Patan. The route takes you past numerous *chaityas* and shrines and, because of its higher elevation, offers a wider view of the Himalayas on clear days. Both villages are situated on terraced hillsides that gradually slope down to the Bagmati. The wooded Chandragiri Mountain rises across the

river. The lovely grove of the Karya Binayak Temple crowns a hill between the two villages.

Kokonah houses about 3,000 Newars in largely traditional-style brick homes. A pagoda temple to the village patroness Rudrayani, one of the Mother Goddesses, dominates the center. Kokonah enjoys a reputation for fine mustard oil and to observe one of the many oil-pressing operations here is to take a peek at pre-industrial technology in full swing.

A short distance further the road ends at Bungamati. The entrance path takes you past ponds, brick and tile houses, small shrines and statues before turning up to the village's primary attraction: the Temple of Red Machhendranath. Since 1533, this *shikhara*-style stone temple has been the summer home of the God of Compassion, who resides in Patan in winter. He is taken to Bungamati at the conclusion of his chariot festival, an event celebrated by a fair graced by one of the rare visits of the Bungamati Kumari.

THECHO, CHAPAGAON, TIKA BHAIRAB. Directly south of Lagankhel runs a second artery from the Ring Road, an unmetalled road running due south. About 3 kilometers later the road rises slightly to a plateau at Sunkothi, a small Newar settlement. From here on, the mountain vistas are excellent. Thecho is the next village of size, slightly larger, with pagoda temples erected to the Mother Goddesses Brahmayani and Balkumari.

Another kilometer south lies a more interesting Newar village, Chapagaon. The network of canals and brick water channels are a working example of Malla Era engineering, a little-appreciated achievement of Nepal's history because the 1934 earthquake destroyed so much of the system. Just east of the village stands a grove sacred to the goddess Vajravarahi, whose 1665 pagoda temple marks the shady center. The woods are a popular picnic spot.

Beyond Chapagaon, the road climbs out of the Valley; it affords several mountain views along the way before dropping into the Lele Valley. A magnificent Tika Bhairab Temple on the riverbank here was swept away by a horrific flood several years ago. The site is still venerated, however, and provides a common stopover for Nepalese coming on foot from the Inner Terai to the Valley.

GODAVARI AND PULCHOWKI. From the same Ring Road junction a third road, this one paved, leads 20 kilometers to Pulchowki Mountain in the southeast corner of the Valley. The village of Godavari lies near the base not far from a sacred water tank which hosts a grand assemblage of pilgrims every 12 years. The area's main feature is a Botanical Garden of numerous exotic plants and flowers. There's a small fish pond close by and a trail that leads up the side of Pulchowki.

This "Flower-covered Hill," a towering 2,762 meter (9,062 feet), is the tallest in the Valley. The trail passes a shrine to the mountain goddess and winds through cool forests replete with songbirds. Goddess Pulchowki is further honored with a temple at the peak where the surrounding view stretches from the plains of the Terai to the mountains of Tibet.

Travel Notes

Land and People

The Kingdom of Nepal is a landlocked, rectangular-shaped, mountainous country of 145,391 square kilometers (56,139 square miles) on the northern end of the South Asian subcontinent. It is located between latitudes 26 degrees and 30 degrees north and longitudes 80 degrees and 88 degrees east; it is bordered by the Tibet Autonomous Region of the People's Republic of China on the north and India on the east, west and south.

Geographically the country consists of three zones: the flat southern strip of alluvial plain and jungle called the Terai, the hilly midlands belt at an altitude ranging between 600 and 2,500 meters above sea level, and the mountainous north. Eight of the world's ten tallest peaks majestically guard Nepal's northern borders. They include the world's tallest, Mt. Everest, which soars 8,848 meters (29,028 feet); the Nepalese call it Sagarmatha — the "Brow of the Ocean." Geological features range from the flat croplands and thick tropical forests of the south to the gorges, glaciers, moraines and snow peaks of the north.

Of the nation's 15.4 million people, those living in the Terai are generally Indo-Aryans, those in the north Tibeto-Burmans; both groups inhabit the midlands. Their official religion is Hindu and the sovereign is regarded as an incarnation of mighty Lord Vishnu. But Nepal has a long history of tolerance and mutual respect for its Buddhist minorities. Others are permitted to freely practice, but not proselytize, their own faiths.

The Kathmandu Valley cradles 565 square kilometers (218 square miles) of enchanted landscape in the heart of the country. It is the home of 800,000 people; 300,000 live in Kathmandu city alone, another 100,000 reside in neighboring Patan, just across the Bagmati River. Bhaktapur, 13 kilometers east, has a population of 50,000. The three cities were once independent, competing entities, but since the Gorkhali conquest in 1769 Kathmandu has been the capital of unified Nepal.

How to Get There

By Air

Kathmandu is connected by air with Karachi, New Delhi, Varanasi, Patna, Calcutta, Dhaka, Dubai, Male, Rangoon, Bangkok, Hong Kong and Singapore. International carriers with regular flights to Nepal are Royal Nepal Airlines, Bangladesh Biman, Burma Airways, Indian Airlines, Lufthansa, Thai International and Singapore Airlines.

By Road

The most commonly followed land routes are: Varanasi-Gorakhpur-Sonauli checkpost-Bhairawa-Kathmandu; Calcutta or Patna-Birganj-Kathmandu; Darjeeling-Siliguri-Kakarvitta checkpost-Kathmandu; Lhasa-Ghasa-Kodari-Kathmandu. All these routes require a sturdy vehicle. It is also wise to pack some camping gear.

Weather

Overall, the climate of the Kathmandu Valley is mild. In mid-winter, temperatures drop to 0° C by dawn but after a morning fog the days are generally clear and bright. By late February even the morning fog clears off. The weather warms up considerably beginning in April and grows hazy. Temperatures peak at 35° C in the sultry weeks of May and June just before the monsoon. The rains commence in late June with the bulk of it falling during the first month. The rains are more intermittent, usually only at night, from August when the festival cycle resumes. The monsoon peters out by early October and the last two months of the year are the most comfortable. Peak trekking times occur late October through mid-December and February through early April, so plan your itinerary accordingly.

A-Z General Information on the Kathmandu Valley

Airport

The expanded Tribhuvan International Airport is 7 kilometers east of Kathmandu. Taxis demand up to Rs 40 from downtown. Local buses leave hourly from Ratna Park and RNAC runs a few shuttles from its New Road headquarters. Porter service is available at the airport at one rupee per bag (plus whatever you wish to tip). Airport tax on departing international flights is Rs 150 per passenger.

Entry and Customs

All visitors except Indian nationals must possess a valid passport. Visas are good for one month and can be obtained at Nepalese embassies and consulates abroad (Calcutta, New Delhi, Dhaka and Lhasa are the nearest). Visas for one week can be obtained at the airport and land entry points. Either way the fee is U.S.$10. Travelers on one-week visas may renew them for three more weeks free of charge. Renewals for a second month cost Rs 300 or Rs 75 per week. Further renewals cost Rs 600 or Rs 150 per week, but extensions beyond three months must be approved by the Home Ministry. In addition, the visitor who extends a visa must present bank exchange receipts for the equivalent of U.S.$5 for each day of the extension requested. Visas are valid only for those places in the Kingdom connected by motorable road. Excursions into the mountains require a separate trekking permit.

These run Rs 60 per week if you have been in Nepal less than two months and Rs 75 per week if you have been in the country for a longer time. However, trekking permits can be purchased in lieu of ordinary visa extensions. The Immigration Office is in Dilli Bazaar, which is open for application until 1 p.m. daily. There is also an office in Pokhara.

Visitors may bring in small quantities of ordinary duty-free allowances such as alcoholic beverages, cigarettes and perfume. An import license from the Ministry of Foreign Affairs or the Home and Panchayat Ministry is required for firearms and ammunition. Radio transmitters, walkie-talkies and illegal drugs are all prohibited. Upon departure, a reasonable amount of souvenirs and handicrafts, including one carpet, may be exported freely. But antiques and art objects require a certificate from the Archaeology Department. The export of objects more than 100 years old is forbidden. Also proscribed are: precious stones, gold and silver in excess of personal jewelry, animal hides and fangs, wild animals, and illegal drugs. Pets, like Tibetan dogs, may be exported. Foreign currency of more than US$2,000 may not be exported unless you had at least that much declared on your customs form when you entered or can produce receipts that prove that you have transferred of funds from abroad through a local bank.

Buses

Most buses serving the various towns of the Valley leave either from Ratna Park or Shahid Gate. The trolley bus to Bhaktapur departs from below the stadium. Minibuses ply the same routes as the big buses, but neither is likely to start moving until the bus is completely packed. Fares from one city to another are around one to two rupees.

Bicycles

Bicycling is one of the most popular, easy-going and

inexpensive ways of exploring the Valley. Hiring a bike costs between six and ten rupees per day, depending on the quality. Be sure to check your bell, brakes and lock before starting out.

Bookshops

The best sources for books on the Kathmandu Valley, Nepal and South Asia are: Himalayan' Books, opposite the Bhatapur-Thimi minibus stand in Bagh Bazar; Ratna Pustak Bhandar, near the French Cultural Center in Bagh Bazar; and, the Order of Pilgrim's Bookshop in Thamel.

Car Hire

Hertz operates out of the office of Gorkha Travel and Avis out of Yeti Travels. Both offices are located on Durbar Marg.

Clothing

Lightweight cottons will suffice from April through September, but you will need woolens and warmer clothes for the autumn and winter months. Locally-made woolen or cotton shawls are a common item of attire in winter and during the evenings in spring and autumn. For excursions to high altitudes you can buy or rent everything extra you might need from trekking shops in Kathmandu or Pokhara.

Communications

The General Post Office is on Kanti Path near the Bhimsen Tower and is open Sunday through Friday from 10 a.m. to 4 p.m. It includes an office of the Philatelic Association, where you can buy Nepal's beautiful commemorative stamps. Travelers are advised to see that their outgoing mail gets franked, although most big hotels have their own mail drops and assume that responsibility themselves. Next door to the GPO is the Foreign Post Office, which handles incoming and outgoing parcels of 500 grams or more. However, it closes at 2 p.m. Sunday through Thursday and at 1 p.m. on Friday.

The International Telegraph and Telephone Exchange is just down the road from the GPO, opposite the stadium. Most big hotels provide telex services. Local calls can be placed from smaller hotels, restaurants and shops for two to three rupees per call.

Driving

A foreigner must possess a valid international driver's license. Traffic moves on the left side of the road and is quite congested in Kathmandu city. Main connecting roads between the Valley and points beyond are generally in good condition; some routes provide excellent vantage points along the way. Drive carefully, however, because if you hit a human or cow you could end up in jail until a compensation arrangement is worked out.

Electricity
All cities and large towns are completely electrified, more or less. The current is 220 volts/50 cycles. Power outages are brief and usually occur during storms but pack of flashlight.

Emergency Telephone Numbers
Bir Hospital Emergency Room: 221-119.
Emergency Police Flying Squad: 216-998, 216-999.

Gambling
Casino Nepal in the Hotel Soaltee is the only licensed gaming house in the country; it was set up exclusively for visiting foreign nationals. The casino operates 24 hours daily and distributes US$5 play coupons as an enticement. All foreign currency winnings may be legally exported from the country.

Guides and Tour Services
New agencies open up every season. Most are located in the Thamel-Kanti Path-Durbar Marg, and New Road-Basantapur areas. Among the reliable ones are: Menuka Travels and Tours, Thamel; Gorkha Travels, Yeti Travels, Adventure Travel Nepal, Mountain Travel/Tiger Tops, all on Durbar Marg; Shanker Travels and Tours, Lazimpat; Kathmandu Travels and Tours, Ganga Path. Among those specializing in trekking only: Ama Dablam Trekking, Lazimpat; Sherpa Cooperative Trekking, Kamal Pokhari; Nepal Trekking and Natural History Expeditions, New Road; and, Himalayan Journeys, Kanti Path.

Health and Medical Care
The underdevelopment of the country is reflected most keenly in things like health service. But there have been dramatic improvements in recent years and potential visitors need not worry that Nepal might be too unhealthy to enjoy. Of course, you must take elementary precautions: Above all, drink only boiled and filtered water, which is available in all hotels and better restaurants. Eat only cooked vegetables and washed or peeled fruits. Avoid overloading on foods which are unfamiliar. Avoid eating too many greasy, fried foods. And avoid eating hot and cold foods at the same sitting.

Illnesses of various sorts most commonly assail residents and visitors just prior to or during the early monsoon months. However, the Valley itself is well-stocked with a multitude of medicines, both of the Western and indigenous varieties. Additionally, there are two major hospitals: the Bir Hospital on Kanti Path and the Western-staffed United Mission Hospital in Patan. In downtown Kathmandu, you can obtain stool, urine or blood tests, or try remedies from aryuvedic centers and Tibetan physicians. There are also doctors of various types, who generally open their offices from 4 p.m. to 6:30 p.m.

In the mountains the biggest danger is altitude sickness, which becomes possible from heights of 11,000 feet or more. Trekkers who are planning to ascend to extremely high altitudes are advised to take along appropriate remedies for nausea and dizziness that are available in Kathmandu or Pokhara drugstores. A complete description of the symptoms, prevention and treatment of altitude sickness can be found in any of the trekkers' guidebooks available in bookstores, as well as in leaflets available from trekking agencies.

Hotels and Accommodations
Registered hotels add a 10 per cent government tax to their rates. Discounts are sometimes available during the off-season. New hotels seem to open every few months, especially in the Thamel and suburban areas. A selection of the better-known hotels in the Valley includes:

Downtown area

Luxury
Annapurna, Durbar Marg, Tel. 211-711, 211-552.
Yak and Yeti, Durbar Marg, 216-255, 216-635.
Malla, Leknath Marg, 215-320, 215-996.
Shangrila, Lazimpat, 212-345, 216-108.
Shanker, Lazimpat, 215-151, 211-973.

Moderate
Yellow Pagoda, Kanti Path, 215-338, 215-492.
Woodlands, Durbar Marg, 212-683.
Makalu, Pako tole, 213-955, 214-616.
Panorama, Kichhapokhari, 211-502.

Budget
Blue Diamond, Thamel, 213-392.
Star, Thamel, 211-004, 216-161.
Kathmandu Guest House, Thamel, 213-628.

Outside the City

Luxury
Soaltee, Kalimati, 211-211, 211-106, 214-213.
Everest Sheraton, Arniko Rajpath, 216-338/339.

Moderate
Dwarika's Village, Battispatuli, 213-770.
Narayani, Pulchowk, Patan, 521-711, 521-442.
Taragaon Village, Boudhanath, 215-413.
Vajra, Bijeswori, 214-545.

Budget
Nyatapola Inn, Taumadhi, Bhaktapur.

Hours and Time
Nepal is 15 minutes ahead of Indian Standard Time and 5 hours, 45 minutes ahead of Greenwich Mean

Time. The Western calendar is used in Nepal, but the official calendar is the Bikram Sambat Era, which began in BC 57; each new year starts on April 13, occasionally April 14. Thus AD 1988 is the equivalent of BS 2045. To further confuse the issue, there is also the unofficial Newari lunar calendar, which most festivals follow and which inaugurates the new year during the new moon of October/November, and the Tibetan calendar which starts during the new moon of Februrary/March. Government offices are open Sunday through Thursday 10 a.m. to 4 p.m. in winter and up to 5 p.m in summer. On Fridays things shut down at 3 p.m. Embassies and international organizations close on Sundays as well. Markets stay open until 7 p.m. at least, but most establishments, restaurants included, close by 11 p.m. Plan on early nights and mornings.

Languages

The national language is Nepalese, an Indo-Aryan, Sanskrit-based tongue which utilizes the Devanagri script common to related North Indian languages. Newari, a Tibeto-Burman language quite different from Nepalese, is the mother-tongue of the Newars of the Kathmandu Valley. Although it boasts a classical literature of its own, written in ancient alphabets, Newari today uses the same Devanagri script and employs many Nepalese words. Tamang, Gurung and their parent tongue Tibetan are also commonly used though most men throughout the Valley speak Nepalese as well. English is understood to varying degrees by the educated and is the lingua franca of tourist shops and the travel trade industry. A growing number of guides and agents are multilingual and Nepalese of all types enjoy trying out their linguistic abilities.

Libraries

The Kaiser Mahal on Kanti Path houses a private collection of 35,000 volumes, including rare Sanskrit texts. Books may be examined on the premises and even photocopied. Other reading libraries open to foreigners are:
The British Council, Kanti Path, weekdays 10-5;
The French Cultural Center, Bagh Bazaar, weekdays 9-12, 3-6;
The Indian Sanskrit Library, RNAC Building, New Road, weekdays 1-6; and,
The Chinese Library, Ganga Path, open Sunday through Friday from 10-4.

Media and Movies

The Rising Nepal is the only English-language daily newspaper. Its office is next to the New Road branch of Nepal Bank Ltd. and its broad sheets are often posted on the wall in the small park in front of the bank. It is distributed to all hotels and available at the newsstands under the pipal tree on New Road. Local and Indian newspapers and magazines are sold here and in the shop in the left-turn lane one block east of the tree. Other international newspapers and magazines are available in big hotels and bookshops.

Radio Nepal broadcasts English news at 8 a.m. and 8 p.m. You can also pick up the BBC and Voice of America at 7:45 a.m. and All-India Radio English news at 9:15 p.m. There are only a handful of cinemas, all showing Hindi or Nepalese films. Videos of Hindi and foreign films compete for customers in the crowded lane that leads north just before the Pashupati temple near Makhan tole. Videos of foreign films are shown at Flo's in Maharajganj, a half-kilometer south of the Ring Road, on the east side down the lane with the huge mirrors on the wall. Call 413-602.

Money Matters

The unit of currency is the Nepalese rupee, consisting of 100 paisa. Coins come in denominations of 5, 10, 25, and 50 paisa and one rupee. Paper currency is issued in notes of Rs 1, 2, 5, 10, 20, 50, 100, 500 and 1000. Banks and registered hotels only are authorized to exchange foreign currency. Ask for and retain receipts, because you will need them when extending visas or exchanging leftover rupees upon your departure. However, only 15 per cent of what you have exchanged may be converted back into dollars when you leave. The Nepal Bank Exchange at the east end of New Road near the Rana Gate keeps later hours than the banks, which are only open for business 10 a.m. to 2 p.m. American Express credit cards are honored at all big hotels and some restaurants and shops. Its office is located on Jamal tole, around the corner from Durbar Marg. Eurocard and VISA are accepted to a lesser extent.

Motorcycles

Rent is on an hourly or per diem basis. Usual rates are Rs 250 to 300 per day. You must have a valid international license and the driver must wear a helmet, which comes with the bike.

Museums

The National Museum is located in Chhauni, one kilometer south of Swayambhunath, and houses a collection of early stone and metal sculptures, paintings, books and various artifacts. Inside Hanuman Dhoka in Basantapur there's a memorial museum devoted to a display of the life and triumphs of King Tribhuvan, who delivered the country from the Rana autocrats in 1951.

Swayambhunath has a small sculpture museum at the southwest corner of the compound. The Natural History Museum is on the southern slope, just above the road. The fauna of the Himalayas make up the exhibits is a good place to familiarize yourself with the appearance of Nepal's wildlife before you go off to the national parks.

Inside the courtyard with the Golden Gate entrance in Patan's Durbar Square is the Metal Arts Museum which has exquisite examples of the city's artisans' mastery of the "lost wax" process of metal casting. Bhaktapur's National Art Gallery in Durbar Square includes many interesting painted manuscripts and *thangkas* among its selections. In Dattatreya Square the beautifully-restored Pujahari Math of Peacock Window fame houses the woodcarving museum. Opposite to it the Chikanpha Math exhibits brass and bronze utensils and artworks.

Nightlife
Kathmandu is not exactly a hotbed of nightlife. Besides videos at Flo's and gambling at the casino, there are only a few places for the restless and sociable. Popular bars include Point 8, next to Nepal Bank New Road; Nanglo's on Durbar Marg; and, Rum Doodle and Spam's Spot, both in Thamel. Disco at Pumpkins, Everest-Sheraton, nightly except Mondays (Tel. 216-388.)

Public Holidays and Festivals
Because of its ethnic diversity and strong dedication to religious practice, Nepal is blessed with a colorful array of festivals. This holds true throughout the country, but is no more apparent than in the Kathmandu Valley, where the Newars alone seem to celebrate something major every month and something minor almost every week. The most popular and widely-observed holidays are:

January
Magh Sakranti — Bathing in sacred river confluences throughout the Valley.

Prithvinarayan Shah's Birthday — A public holiday honoring the founder of the reigning dynasty's rule over Nepal.

Sri Panchami — A homage to the deities of learning, Saraswati and Manjusri, and a day of weddings and other rites of passage that are celebrated for several weeks.

February
Democracy Day — A public holiday that marks the milestone of King Tribhuvan's overthrow of the Rana autocracy in 1951.

Losar — The Tibetan New Year with events at Boudhanath and Swayambhunath; the festivities surrounding it last until March in some years.

Shivaratri — Bathing in honor of Shiva at Pashupatinath attracts pilgrims by the thousands and Indian sadhus; bonfires are built at night; bring your blanket.

Holi — A wild Hindu festival lasting into March that involves the throwing of water bags and colored powder among other merrymaking.

March
Ghoda Jatra — Horse races and shows in Tundikhel Parade Ground coincide with the Newar Pisach Chaturdasi; feasts and rites include masked dancers who drink the blood of dying sacrificial victims. Not recommended for the faint-hearted or animal lovers.

April
Bisket — Bhaktapur celebrates the New Year for nine days with chariot processions, the erection of a gigantic pole, exhibitions of local deities and feasts.

Bal Kumari Jatra — Thimi celebrates the New Year with a morning procession of 16 deities and the hurling of orange powder.

Red Machhendranath Chariot Festival — Patan's red-faced God of Compassion takes a grand chariot tour of the city, accompanied by Minnath's car; the festivities continue until June.

May
Buddha Jayanti — Marks the Buddha's day of birth, enlightenment and death, celebrated with dances, displays and processions.

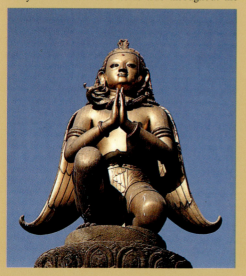

July
Ghantakarna — A sacred month for the Newars; wee hour procession to Swayambhunath and Adinath, Buddhist rituals and image displays lasting into August.

August
Janai Purnima — Sacred threads are reissued to upper caste Hindus; Tamang shamans visit Patan's Kumbheswar Temple; there are also pilgrimages to Gosainkund to make offerings.

Gai Jatra — A procession is held in honor of those who have died since the previous year; people don hilarious costumes; in Bhaktapur, there are nine nights of masked dances, skits in the streets and mass processions.

September
Teej — A fast is held and there is a bathing ritual for Brahmin-Chetri women at Pashupati.

Indra Jatra — Spectacular chariot processions of Ganesh, Bhairab and the Living Goddess Kumari are held in the presence of His Majesty the King; a week of masked dances, processions, rituals and nightly pageant presentations.

October
Dasain — Nationwide celebrations in honor of Durga's victory over the evil demons, with nightly rounds of shrines in Bhaktapur and masked dances in Patan, animals sacrifices, processions of gods and sword-dancers and Kumaris.

Tihar or Diwali — The Festival of Lights; houses are illuminated and there are special rites for crows, dogs, cows, bulls, and younger brothers; the Newar New Year is also celebrated.

November
Birthday of Her Majesty Queen Ashwariya Raja Laxmi Devi Shah.

Kartik Purnima — A full moon harvest festival that includes masked dances in some villages and grain displays in religious pictures at Bhaktapur.

December
Yomarhi Punhi — A full moon post-harvest festival during which rice cakes are distributed and masked dances are held in some southern villages.

Birthday of His Majesty King Birendra Bir Bikram Shah Dev.

Religious Services
Roman Catholic: St. Xavier's, Jawalakhel, Patan, Tel. 52150; also held at Annapurna Hotel, Durbar Marg, 211711.
Protestant: USIS, Rabi Bhavan, 213996.
Jewish: Israeli Embassy, 211251.
Muslim: Shahi Jama Masjid, easily identifiable on the lower side of Durbar Marg.

Restaurants

Big hotels have their own restaurants with both Asian and Western menus. Most of the better restaurants are in the Thamel or Durbar Marg areas. It's a fast expanding service industry, with competition forcing up the quality and variety. Among the most reputable, by type are:

Nepalese and Tibetan
Sunkosi, Durbar Marg.
Tibet's Kitchen, Chetrapati.

Indianstyle
Gharekabab, Durbar Marg.
Amber, Durbar Marg.

Vegetarian
Tripti's, opposite Cosy Hotel, off New Road (Indian).
Paradise, Jhochhe tole (Western).

Italian
La Dolce Vita, Thamel.
Marco Polo, Thamel.

Korean
Arirang, Durbar Marg.

Japanese
Fuji, Kanti Path.
Koto, Durbar Marg.

Chinese
Golden Gate, Kanti Path.
Nanglo's, Durbar Marg.

Shopping

For foreign visitors, handicrafts dominate the markets. Common purchases include carpets, ready-made clothing, votive objects, paintings, jewelry, pashmina shawls and other textiles. In Kathmandu the main bazaars are on the diagonal route from Makhan tole to Kanti Path. Thamel, Durbar Marg, New Road and Jhochhe tole-Basantapur. In Patan they are mainly clustered in and around Mangal Bazar and the Tibetan Refugee Center in south Jawalakhel. In Bhaktapur the shops catering to foreigners are in the Durbar Square-Taumadhi area and in Dattatreya Square. The latest contemporary fashions and gadgets from Bangkok and Hong Kong can be found in the Supermarket and shops on and branching off New Road. Nepalese shopowners generally do not add a high markup to their goods, which means you are unlikely to be charged outrageous prices; but you cannot bargain prices down much either. You can haggle, however, with those selling goods in the layouts located all along the streets of Kathmandu. Always be on the lookout for the unusual; you will be certain to find it somewhere in Kathmandu.

Sports

Golfers can play on either of two nine-hole courses, one at Gokarna Forest, the other near the airport. For details call the Royal Nepal Golf Club at 412836. Five-star hotels like Soaltee and Yak and Yeti will sell memberships to non-guests for the use of their swimming pools and tennis courts. The National Stadium also has a tennis court and swimming pool and there are squash courts at the Oasis Club at Hotel Narayani in Patan. There's a well-equipped Kathmandu Physical Centre just before the Shanker Hotel turnoff.

Taboos and Customs

Being polite people themselves, the Nepalese appreciate the same quality in others. There are only a few extraordinary rules to remember. The *"namaste"* greeting is made with the hands folded chest high and the head slightly bowed. Some Westernized Nepalese are enthusiastic handshakers, others are not. The right hand is the clean hand, the only one with which you offer anything, but you should never offer anything from a cup or bowl which you are using for your own food or drink. If you are invited into a Nepalese home for a meal, your hosts will probably eat with their hands, but more than likely will offer you utensils. Public displays of affection between members of the opposite sex never occur and foreigners should refrain also from them, but handholding and embracing between members of the same sex is not uncommon so don't look surprised.

Taxis, Scooters and Rickshaws

Latest taxi rates start at Rs 1.80 and click off 60 paisa every half kilometer. In foul weather and after dark drivers usually insist on bargaining rather than using the meter. Rates for a full day of touring depend upon the terrain and distance, but expect to pay at least Rs 300. It is better to fix it from your hotel or a travel agent. An alternative to regular taxis are the scooter cabs, which are slightly cheaper and fit up to three passengers. Last are the gaudy cycle rickshaws. Bargain and settle the fare before you start your ride.

Theft

Hotels will check your valuables safely for you. Armed robbery is extremely rare, but pickpockets work the city buses and the festival crowds; photographers are special targets. If you plan to mingle with the crowds, use common sense. Don't wade in with a fat wallet bulging in your pocket,

keep your gear secure and have fun. Thievery does plague the post office, especially the Poste Restante section. Do not have cash, checks, and other valuables sent to you by mail. Use the banking system instead. When trekking, don't flash your money around if you want to keep it.

Tourist Information Offices

The Kathmandu office is on Ganga Path, just before Basantapur Square. The Pokhara office is a few minutes' walk from the airstrip towards the lakeside. Check the latest brochures here.

Weights and Measures

The metric system is widely understood and the educated and those in the travel trade industry can make sense of the English system. The Indian terms lakh (100,000) and crore (100 lakhs or 10 million) are commonly quoted. Local shop terms include:
Jewelry: 1 tola = 11.6 grams; 1 carat = .2 gram.
Produce: 1 pau = 200 grams; 1 dharni = 12 pau, or 2.4 kilograms.
Liquids, grains: 1 mana = slightly under ½ liter, 1 paathi = 8 mana or c. 3 and ¾ liters, 1 muri = 20 paathi or 75 liters.

Useful Vocabulary

English	Nepalese
Hello, goodbye	*Namaste*
Thank you.	*Dhanyabad.*
Excuse me.	*Maphi garnos.*
How are you?	*Tapainle kasto cha?*
How much?	*Kati?*
My name is . . .	*Mero nam . . . ho.*
Where is your home?	*Tapainko ghar kahan ho?*
yes, no	*ho, hoina*
I don't know.	*Tha chaina.*
Please come in.	*Bhitra aunos.*
Please sit down.	*Basnos.*
my, your, his/her	*mero, tapainko, usko*
today, tomorrow	*aja, bholi*
yesterday	*hijo*
the day after tomorrow	*parsi*
What time is it?	*Kati bajyo?*
who, when	*ki, kahile*
where, why	*kahan, kina*
what, which	*ke, kun*
left, right	*baya, daya*
straight	*sidhaa*
like this	*tyesto*
Speak slowly.	*Bistaare bholnos.*
sick	*biraami*
hot water	*tato pani*
cold water	*chiso pani*
good/beautiful	*ramro*
hot, cold	*garma, jado*
delicious	*mitho*
clean, dirty	*safa, mailo*
I don't understand.	*Milai bujhdaina*
take, give	*linos, dinos*
Where are you going?	*Kahan jane?*
bring	*lyaunos*
big, small	*thulo, saano*
have, have not	*chha, chhaina*
much, many	*dherai*
medicine	*ausadhi*

Index

A
accommodation (see hotels)
airport (Tribhuvan International Airport), 96
Annapurna Sanctuary, 88
art gallery, 68, 69
Arun Valley, 88

B
Bagmati River, *15*
Basantapur Palace, *24, 40*
Bhairab (patron deity), *35*
Bhaktapur, 14
bookshops, 68, 97
Boudhanath, 84
Buddhism, 34
Buddhist meditation courses, 68
buses, 97

C
Café, Nyatapola, 82
Cave, Mahendra, 86
Chitwan (see parks)

D
Dakshinkali, Black Goddess, 55
deities, *36, 37, 51*
Devi dancers, *54*
Durbar Square, *24*, 75, 77

F
Festivals, 100, 101
 Gai Jatra, *32*, 67
 Horse, *6-7*
 Kumari Chariot, 42

G
Goddess Kumari, *49*
Golden Gate, 81
Gurkha soldiers, *40, 47*

H
handicrafts
 carpets, 58, 69
 fabrics, 68, 69
 woodcarving, 68, 69
health and medical care, 98
hotel, 98

K
Kings
 Birenda, 46
 Jayaprakash, *25*
 Mahendra, *27, 28*, 46
 Tribhuvan, *22*, 46
Kumari House, 75

L
Lakes
 Gosainkund, 88
 Phewa, *20*
 Rara, 89
libraries, 99
Lumbini pilgrimage site, 91

M
Malla era, 37
Maps
 Bhaktapur, *80*
 Kathmandu Old Town, *72-3*
 Kathmandu Valley, *64-5*
 Patan, *78*
 Pokhara, *85*
Monasteries
 Boudhanath, *8-9*
 Buddhist Chaturvarna Vihar, 81
 monk, *48*
Mountains
 Everest, 88
 Fishtail, 86
 Lantang, 88
 Makalu, 88
 Solo Khumbu, 88
Museums, 99
 National, 77
 National History, 77

N
Namche Bazaar, 88
National flag, 67
Nature Trail, 84
Newars, 51, *52*, 54, 55

P
Pagoda, Kasthamandap, 75
Parks
 Gokarna Forest Safari Park, 84, 86
 Royal Bardia National Park, 91
 Royal Chitwan National Park, 90
Patan, 14, 67
people, *52-3*
Pokhara Valley, *21*, 84
prayer-wheel, *56*
public holidays, 100, 101
puja rites, 13, 21, 57

R
rakshi (spirit), 57, 67
restaurants, 102
rites and ceremonies, *54, 55*
Royal Palace, 81

S
sadhus, *30, 31*, 66
shopping, 102
shrines, *43*, 83, 95
 Mahakali, 82, 83
 Mahalaxmi, 82
 Manjusri, 77
 Pashupatinath, 83
 Shantipur, 77
 Swayambhunath, 76
 Varahi, 83
sports, 102

T
taboos and customs, 102
Temples
 Adko Narayan, 75
 Annapurna, 76
 Batsala Durga, 81
 Bhairab, *62, 82*
 Bhimsen, 86
 Bhubaneshwari, 83
 Bindabasini, 86
 Boudhanath, *42*
 Chhoche Ganesh, 82
 Dattatreya, 82
 Degu Talle, 79
 Devi, 83
 Itum Bahal, 76
 Kankeswari, 76
 Krishna, 83
 Kumbheswar, 79
 Kwa Bahal, 79
 Mahaboudha, 77
 Minnath, 77
 Muktinath, 88
 Nava Durga, 82
 Nyatapola, 82
 Pashupatinath, *30*, 81
 Rajeswari, *16-17*
 Shiva, 83
 Sitala Ajima, 76
 Surya Binayak, 83
 Taleju, 75
 Wakupati Narayan, 82
thangkas (scrolls), 68, 69, *70*
Thimi village, 83
tours, 69, 98
transport, 97, 102
trekking, 88, 89, 90, 91

V
Valley Trivia, 66
Varahi *dyogha*, 82
Vishu, *14*, 46, 194

W
waterfall (Patala Chhango), 87
weather, 96
woodcarving, *38, 39*

Y
Yamdi Valley, 87
yeti, 66

Acknowledgements

It is impossible to thank all those who have been of assistance to the author throughout his studies in Nepal, but to mention the most obvious: Ashok Jangam, long-time partner in the exploration of things Nepalese; Ian Alsop and Goetz Hagmueller for continuous historical and cultural insights; Maggie and Vikki Floyd for their constant support and encouragement through the years; Basudev and Vishnu Hari for their gracious hospitality; Kiran Man Chitrakar and M.K. Gupta for the historical photos; and Rolf Kluenter for the copy work; and, Gagendra Chettri Menuka Travels and Tours for the Travel Information.

Additional Photo Credits

Prints by **Oldfield** (1851-53): 24
M.K. Gupta: 27, 28
From the collection of **Kiran Man Chitrakar,**
Ganesh Photo, Kathmandu: 22, 23, 29
Jim Goodman: 58-59
From the collection of **Ian Alsop:** 25